OCCASIONAL PAPER 122

Capital Flows in the APEC Region

Edited by Mohsin S. Khan and Carmen M. Reinhart

INTERNATIONAL MONETARY FUND
Washington DC
March 1995

Library of Congress Cataloging-in-Publication Data

Capital flows in the APEC region / edited by Mohsin S. Khan and Carmen
    M. Reinhart.
        p.   cm. — (Occasional Papers, ISSN 1251-6365 ; 122)
        Background papers prepared by IMF staff for meetings of APEC
(Asia Pacific Economic Cooperation Council) region ministers.
        ISBN 1-55775-466-7
        1. Capital movements—Asia.   2. Capital movements—Pacific Area.
I. Khan, Mohsin S.   II. Reinhart, Carmen M.   III. International
Monetary Fund.   IV. Asia Pacific Economic Cooperation (Organization)
V. Series: Occasional paper (International Monetary Fund) ; no. 122.
HG3891.C368   1995
332'.042—dc20   95-6419
                                                                              CIP

Price: US$15.00
(US$12.00 to full-time faculty members and
students at universities and colleges)

Please send orders to:
International Monetary Fund, Publication Services
700 19th Street, N.W., Washington, D.C. 20431, U.S.A.
Tel.: (202) 623-7430   Telefax: (202) 623-7201
Internet: publications@imf.org

recycled paper

Contents

Preface

This Occasional Paper contains a set of papers dealing with various aspects of capital inflows in the Asia-Pacific Economic Cooperation Council (APEC) region. These papers were prepared by IMF staff in response to requests made by the APEC Ministers of Finance. One of the papers, "Macroeconomic Management in APEC Economies: The Response to Capital Inflows," was prepared as background for the joint ministerial meeting held in Honolulu, Hawaii (March 18–19, 1994), while the other two were considered at the meeting of APEC Deputy Finance Ministers in Madrid, Spain (October 3, 1994).

The authors of the papers received useful comments from staff in other departments. They are grateful to Anne Jansen, Jared Romey, and Subramanian S. Sriram for research assistance and to Norma Alvarado, Darlene Alvis, Lucia Buono, Ann-Barbara Hyde, and Tammi Shear for secretarial assistance. Elisa Diehl of the External Relations Department edited the manuscript and coordinated the publication process.

The opinions expressed in the papers are those of the authors and do not necessarily reflect the views of the IMF or its Executive Directors.

I Introduction

The developing economies of the Asia-Pacific Economic Cooperation Council (APEC) have been the recipients of a considerable volume of capital inflows in the 1990s.[1] For example, in 1993 capital inflows to the APEC countries accounted for about 85 percent of the capital that went to developing economies. In some cases, such as Malaysia and Thailand, the inflows have on occasion amounted to as much as 15 percent of GDP. Not surprisingly, there has emerged among policy circles in these countries a considerable interest in understanding the causes, patterns, and nature of these international capital flows, as well as the effect that this surge would have on economic activity, relative prices, the banking system, and the stock market.

The issue of whether the inflows were primarily driven by sound domestic policies and market-oriented reforms—the "pull" factors—or declining international interest rates and poor returns in stock markets in industrial countries—the "push" factors—became a focal point of the policy discussions. If external conditions played a key role in inducing the inflows, it has been argued, then there is cause for greater caution, as a change in the international environment could prompt a reversal of the flows. On the other hand, if these inflows were responding primarily to conditions in the recipient countries, there is less reason to be concerned about swift reversals. Policies would thus need to be set according to which factors appeared dominant.

These sizable inflows were also having important macroeconomic effects; they were helping finance higher investment and growth, but there was also a tendency for the nominal and real exchange rate to appreciate and the current account to worsen. Given the increased integration of capital markets, it is not surprising to find that for many developing APEC economies monetary control became more difficult, particularly as the inflows persisted and an increasing share of inflows came in the form of short-term capital.

Concerns also emerged that the banking system was not always adequately intermediating the inflows and that the stock market may have become more volatile as the role of foreign investors increased. Hence, formulating an appropriate policy response to these developments has naturally been an important issue during the early 1990s for the countries concerned and for the international community at large. The three papers that make up this Occasional Paper each examine different aspects of these issues.

Section II, "Portfolio Capital Flows to the Developing Country Members of APEC," focuses on the pattern of capital flows to the APEC developing countries in recent years, analyzing the trends and describing the composition of the flows. The emphasis is on portfolio flows, which account for an increasingly important share of capital movements to these countries. Indeed, international issuance of bonds and equities by emerging market economies, most of which are APEC countries, reached unprecedented proportions in 1991–93. Hence, Section II examines the characteristics of international transactions in bonds and equities. With regard to the sources of the inflows, it provides a brief analysis of the investor base as well as presenting some indications of the destination of these capital flows at both the macroeconomic and microeconomic level.

The possible causes and macroeconomic effects of the surge in inflows are examined in Section III, "Macroeconomic Management in APEC Economies: The Response to Capital Inflows." This section reviews the recent debate as to whether the inflows are primarily driven by sound domestic policies and an attractive investment climate or by external factors, such as interest rate developments in the United States. The issue remains particularly timely, given the increase in interest rates in the United States in 1994 and the current expectation that further increases are likely to follow. Section III analyzes the impact of the inflows on international reserves, the current account, the real exchange rate, and investment and growth. Where relevant, the experience of the APEC countries is compared to other developing countries that have also experienced a surge in capital inflows. The section concludes with a discussion of the relative merits of a variety of monetary, exchange rate, fiscal, and structur-

---

[1]The developing economies of APEC include the following: Brunei, China, Hong Kong, Indonesia, Korea, Malaysia, Mexico, Papua New Guinea, the Philippines, Singapore, Taiwan Province of China, and Thailand. The APEC industrial countries include Australia, Canada, Japan, New Zealand, and the United States. Chile became a member in 1994.

al policies, such as capital account liberalization, that have often been implemented in these countries in response to the surge in inflows.

Section IV, "Effect of Capital Flows on the Domestic Financial Sectors in APEC Developing Countries," analyzes the effect that sizable and often volatile capital inflows have on the domestic financial sectors in APEC developing countries. On the banking side, the emphasis is on assessing the ability of the banking systems in the recipient countries to intermediate the inflows adequately by satisfactorily assessing, pricing, and managing risk. Since sterilized intervention has been the policy most often implemented in the capital-importing countries, the section describes the various forms this policy has taken and analyzes how sterilized intervention affects the banking system and the financial sector at large. The adequacy of the regulatory and supervisory framework is examined in light of its intended role in containing systemic risk, particularly in the event of a reversal in capital flows. Furthermore, since much of the inflows have been funneled through the stock market, often leading to booms in these emerging markets, this section also investigates whether the surge in inflows has increased the volatility of stock prices in the emerging markets in the APEC region. The issues of whether the increased international capital flows have given rise to increased pricing inefficiencies and/or have led to increased "spillover" effects from the equity markets in industrial countries are also addressed.

II   Portfolio Capital Flows to the Developing Country Members of APEC

Shogo Ishii and Steven Dunaway

Over the past five years, developing countries as a whole have experienced a strong increase in capital inflows, as many of these countries have implemented strong macroeconomic and structural reform programs and have resolved their debt problems. No other group of countries within this broad category has witnessed as large an increase in private capital inflows as the developing country members of the Asia-Pacific Economic Cooperation Council (APEC), and, indeed, inflows to this group have dominated developments in such flows to the developing world.

This section focuses on flows to the developing country members of APEC, analyzing recent trends and the composition and characteristics of international transactions in bonds and equities. It also presents some indications of the sources and destinations of these capital flows. However, serious data limitations limit the analysis. Balance of payments data are not available for Brunei and Hong Kong, with the lack of data for Hong Kong being especially important. Available balance of payments data also do not provide substantial details on the geographic origins and destinations of international capital transactions. Particularly in the case of portfolio capital flows, only limited data are available on bilateral transactions. An additional complication is the role played by international and regional financial centers as intermediaries in portfolio capital transactions, making it more difficult to track capital flows from their source to their ultimate destination. Information on types of portfolio transactions is also incomplete. While data on international placements of bond and equity issues are plentiful, only limited data are available on direct purchases by foreigners of securities on local financial markets. In addition, only partial information is available on the composition and characteristics of the investors in the securities of the APEC developing countries and on the recipients of this funding in these countries. Where gaps in the available information exist, partial or indicative data are used to illustrate developments and basic trends. All in all, there probably exist significant unrecorded capital flows.

Recent Experience

Following the onset of the debt crisis in 1982, medium- and long-term capital flows to developing coun-

tries as a group fell sharply, with net outflows taking place during 1987–88 (Chart 2-1).[2] In 1990, the flows began to rebound strongly and have since risen rapidly, with the composition shifting substantially over the period. While syndicated bank loans had been the principal sources in the 1970s and early 1980s, foreign direct investment and portfolio capital flows have accounted for most of the inflows in the 1990s. The majority of these flows have gone to a relatively small number of countries concentrated in Asia and Latin America, most of them APEC members. In fact, the developing country members of APEC were the destination of a very high proportion of total medium- and long-term capital flows to developing countries during 1990–93 (Table 2-1 and Appendix Table 1; appendix tables begin on p. 58).

There was a slowdown in capital inflows in early 1994 following increases in U.S. interest rates beginning in February. Private financing for developing countries in the form of portfolio flows posted a steep drop. Even the developing country members of APEC with relatively good credit ratings experienced a tightening in the terms on new bond issues and significant declines in stock prices. Given the prevailing uncertainties, both issuers and investors in bonds and stocks pulled back and waited for the markets to settle. In May and June 1994, the return of some high-quality issuers to the markets indicated a modest recovery.

Composition and Geographic Distribution of Capital Flows

The rapid rise in medium- and long-term capital flows to APEC developing countries since the late

---

[2]These medium- and long-term flows include foreign direct investment, portfolio investment (bond and equity transactions), and other long-term capital flows to the private sector and to public sector enterprises. The distinction between portfolio equity flows and foreign direct investment equity flows is based on standard balance of payments accounting definitions. Foreign direct investment equity flows represent investments by residents of one country in the equities of a firm that is resident in another country, with the investors having the intention of exerting a direct influence on the operations of the firm. In the balance of payments accounts, this intention is defined in terms of a foreign resident acquiring a 10 percent or greater equity stake in a domestic firm.

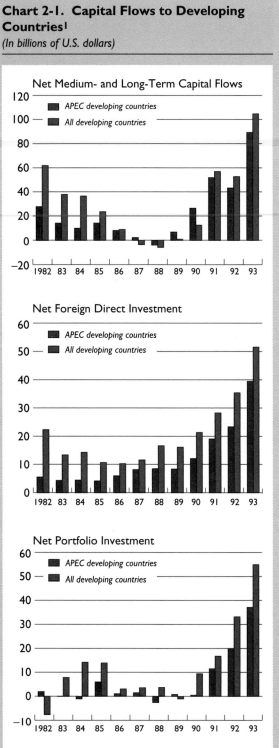

Chart 2-1. Capital Flows to Developing Countries¹
(In billions of U.S. dollars)

Net Medium- and Long-Term Capital Flows

■ APEC developing countries
■ All developing countries

Net Foreign Direct Investment

■ APEC developing countries
■ All developing countries

Net Portfolio Investment

■ APEC developing countries
■ All developing countries

Sources: IMF, *Balance of Payments Statistics Yearbook* (Washington, various issues); and IMF staff estimates.
¹Net medium- and long-term capital, excluding exceptional financing and flows associated with debt- and debt-service-reduction operations; Brunei and Hong Kong are not included owing to the unavailability of data.

1980s primarily reflects the strong growth in foreign direct investment and a dramatic increase in portfolio capital inflows (Chart 2-2 and Table 2-2). Other capital flows (primarily bank lending) shifted from net outflows in the mid-1980s back to net inflows following the resolution of the debt problems of some APEC members in the late 1980s. Nonetheless, such flows have not been a consistent source of funding, partly reflecting the cautious attitude of commercial banks toward new lending to developing countries.

The pattern of capital inflows to the different subgroups of APEC developing countries has varied significantly (Chart 2-3). Most of the inflows in recent years have gone to Mexico and to the Asian APEC members other than the newly industrializing economies (NIEs). For Mexico, this represents a sharp reversal of the experience during the 1980s, when debt difficulties were manifested in net capital outflows during most of the period after 1982. With the resolution of debt problems and restoration of confidence associated with the implementation of sound policies, Mexico has witnessed a dramatic rise in capital inflows during the 1990s. In contrast, the Asian members of APEC other than the NIEs received significant capital inflows throughout the 1980s, with a marked increase taking place in the early 1990s. Capital flows to the Asian NIEs generally declined over the 1980s and into the 1990s, as some of these countries have begun to provide funds, particularly to other countries in the region.

Foreign direct investment has been a significant source of financing for APEC developing countries (Chart 2-4 and Appendix Table 2). Inflows to these countries grew in the second half of the 1980s and rose sharply in the early 1990s, as the non-NIE Asian countries implemented economic policies and structural reforms that led to an improved investment climate. Flows of foreign direct investment to China rose rapidly, along with a pickup in such flows to Indonesia, Malaysia, and Thailand. Mexico also experienced a rise in inflow of direct investment but to a lesser extent. In contrast, there have been only modest net inflows of foreign direct investment to the APEC NIEs as a group, largely owing to a shift to net outflows of direct investment capital in the 1990s from Taiwan Province of China, which has become an important source of foreign direct investment, especially for China.

The most significant development in the 1990s, however, has been the growing importance of portfolio capital flows as a means of financing for the developing country members of APEC. Net portfolio capital inflows to these countries have increased from negligible levels during the 1980s (Chart 2-5 and Appendix Table 3) to account for a high and rising portion of total capital inflows during the 1990s. Among the developments that have made the climate for portfolio investment in these countries more attractive are improved foreign access to local financial markets, especially to

Table 2-1. Capital Flows to Developing Countries[1]

	Annual Average 1982–89	1990	1991	1992	1993
	(In billions of U.S. dollars)				
All developing countries	20.1	12.6	57.1	52.7	104.8
APEC developing countries	10.0	26.6	51.9	43.3	89.4
Asia	10.2	13.0	29.8	23.6	57.6
NIEs[2]	−1.7	−5.0	5.1	7.3	8.7
Other	11.9	17.9	24.7	16.3	48.9
Chile	−0.9	0.8	0.5	0.8	1.5
Mexico	0.7	12.8	21.6	18.9	30.3
Other developing countries	15.0	−14.0	5.2	9.4	15.4
	(In percent of GDP)				
All developing countries	0.7	0.3	1.3	1.3	2.3
APEC developing countries	1.2	1.9	3.4	2.5	4.6
Asia	1.5	1.2	2.5	1.8	3.8
NIEs[2]	—	−1.1	1.0	1.3	1.5
Other	2.3	2.8	3.6	2.1	5.3
Chile	−5.1	2.8	1.5	1.9	3.4
Mexico	0.5	5.2	7.5	5.7	8.4
Other developing countries	0.6	−0.5	0.2	0.4	0.6

Sources: IMF, *Balance of Payments Statistics Yearbook*; and IMF staff estimates.

[1]Net medium- and long-term capital, excluding exceptional financing and flows associated with debt- and debt-service-reduction operations; Brunei and Hong Kong are not included owing to the unavailability of data.

[2]Korea, Singapore, and Taiwan Province of China.

stock markets, as well as improved availability and reliability of financial information on domestic firms.

Entities in these countries seeking to tap deeper pools of funds to meet their expanding capital needs for investment have also ventured into international financial markets. At the same time, international investors have shown greater interest in APEC developing countries. With the slowdown in economic activity in the industrial countries and the fall in interest rates worldwide in the early 1990s, developing country securities became more attractive owing to their higher returns. Lower international interest rates also reduced the debt-service burden of these countries and, hence, reduced default risk. Moreover, there appears to have been some reassessment of the riskiness of these securities, particularly for the APEC developing countries, owing in part to the solid macroeconomic policy track records they have established and their generally strong economic performance over the period. Mexico has been the major recipient of portfolio capital inflows during the 1990s, accounting for about 60 percent of these flows to APEC developing countries. Nevertheless, Asian APEC members have also experienced substantial increases in portfolio inflows.

Recent Trends and Characteristics of Portfolio Capital Flows

International bond and equity placements have been a major avenue for portfolio flows to APEC developing countries, expanding noticeably in the early 1990s and reaching $39 billion in 1993 (Chart 2-6).[3] Both the investor base (especially with added institutional investor interest) and the range of borrowers with access to private market financing broadened considerably. By 1993, all of the larger developing country members of APEC were able to tap both international bond and equity markets. The increase in bond and equity flows to APEC developing countries was led principally by China, Indonesia, Malaysia, Mexico, the Philippines, and Thailand, reflecting investors' recognition of the strength of economic policies and growth prospects in these countries. In the case of Mexico and the Philippines, the normalization of relations with private creditors following the completion of operations to reduce the two countries' debt and debt service also played an important role. Asian APEC NIEs have

---

[3]Data on international placements of bonds include issues by sovereign borrowers; these issues are identified separately in the tables.

Chart 2-2. Composition of Capital Flows to APEC Developing Countries[1]
(In billions of U.S. dollars)

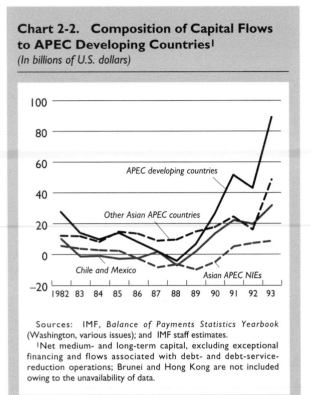

Sources: IMF, *Balance of Payments Statistics Yearbook* (Washington, various issues); and IMF staff estimates.
[1]Net medium- and long-term capital, excluding exceptional financing and flows associated with debt- and debt-service-reduction operations; Brunei and Hong Kong are not included owing to the unavailability of data.

Chart 2-3. Capital Flows to APEC Developing Countries[1]
(In billions of U.S. dollars)

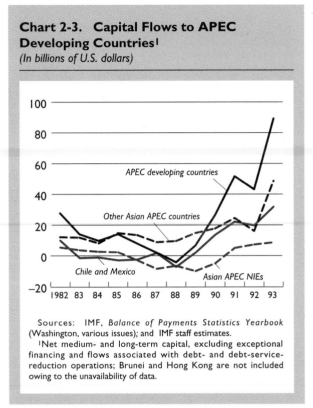

Sources: IMF, *Balance of Payments Statistics Yearbook* (Washington, various issues); and IMF staff estimates.
[1]Net medium- and long-term capital, excluding exceptional financing and flows associated with debt- and debt-service-reduction operations; Brunei and Hong Kong are not included owing to the unavailability of data.

maintained a presence in international bond and equity markets for many years and have stepped up placements of new issues in these markets in the early 1990s to exploit cheaper sources of funding brought about by the decline in international interest rates during this period. The decline in interest rates, along with strong economic policy performance in these countries, improved market perceptions of the creditworthiness

Table 2-2. Capital Flows to APEC Developing Countries[1]

	Annual Average 1982–89	1990	1991	1992	1993
	(In billions of U.S. dollars)				
Capital flows	9.8	26.6	51.9	43.3	89.4
Foreign direct investment	6.2	12.1	19.1	23.4	39.5
Portfolio investment	0.9	0.5	11.5	19.9	37.1
Other	2.7	14.1	21.3	—	12.8
	(In percent)				
Memorandum items:					
Real GDP growth					
All developing countries	4.5	3.7	4.5	6.0	6.2
APEC developing countries	6.6	5.7	7.0	8.7	8.9
Other developing countries	3.2	2.4	2.5	3.7	3.8
Industrial countries	3.0	2.4	0.7	1.5	1.3

Sources: IMF, *Balance of Payments Statistics Yearbook*; IMF, *World Economic Outlook*; and IMF staff estimates.
[1]Net medium- and long-term capital excluding exceptional financing and flows associated with debt- and debt-service-reduction operations; Brunei and Hong Kong are not included owing to the unavailability of data.

Chart 2-4. Net Foreign Direct Investment in APEC Developing Countries¹
(In billions of U.S. dollars)

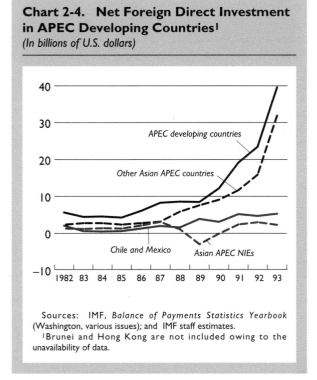

Sources: IMF, *Balance of Payments Statistics Yearbook* (Washington, various issues); and IMF staff estimates.
¹Brunei and Hong Kong are not included owing to the unavailability of data.

Chart 2-5. Net Portfolio Capital Flows to APEC Developing Countries¹
(In billions of U.S. dollars)

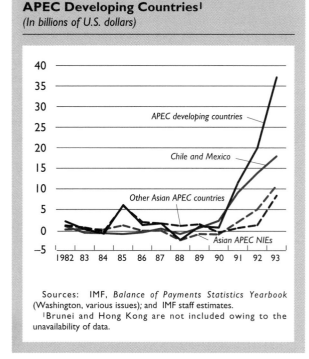

Sources: IMF, *Balance of Payments Statistics Yearbook* (Washington, various issues); and IMF staff estimates.
¹Brunei and Hong Kong are not included owing to the unavailability of data.

Chart 2-6. International Bond and Equity Issues by APEC Developing Countries
(In billions of U.S. dollars)

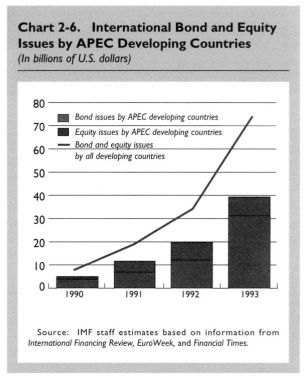

Source: IMF staff estimates based on information from *International Financing Review, EuroWeek,* and *Financial Times.*

of their securities, facilitating access to international financial markets. APEC developing countries' access to international markets was also facilitated by regulatory changes in several creditor countries.[4] Notably, the relaxation of restrictions on private placements in the United States improved access by developing country borrowers to this market.

As noted above, conditions in international financial markets changed significantly in the first half of 1994 with the increases in U.S. interest rates. As a consequence, the volume of international bonds and equities issued by APEC developing countries as a group fell significantly between February and April 1994 from the record levels achieved in the final quarter of 1993. Nonetheless, the decline in placements by APEC developing countries was less steep than for other developing countries overall, owing to the fact that APEC members are generally viewed as being better credit risks. During this turbulent period in the financial markets, both issuers of securities and investors reduced their activities, waiting for conditions to settle. In May and June 1994, some recovery in placements took place, with higher-quality issuers, particularly APEC developing country members, returning to the markets. Despite these recent market developments,

[4]These changes are discussed more fully in *Private Market Financing for Developing Countries*, World Economic and Financial Surveys (Washington: International Monetary Fund, December 1993).

portfolio flows to APEC developing countries in the first half of 1994 were still significantly higher than the levels of the previous three years.

Bonds

In line with the recent trend in flows to other developing countries, the composition of private capital flows to APEC developing countries has shifted toward bond financing during the 1990s. International bonds issued by APEC developing countries increased from $4 billion in 1990 to $31 billion in 1993, partly in response to the decline in U.S. long-term interest rates and growing investor interest in these securities (Chart 2-7 and Appendix Table 4). Local stock market booms in Asian APEC members also made a major contribution to the increase in bond placements, as private firms in these countries expanded their access to funding and lowered their borrowing costs by issuing substantial amounts of bonds that could be converted into equities. Some APEC developing countries, including China and Mexico, issued sizable global bonds to tap several major international markets simultaneously. In so doing, they sought to attract broader demand and thus obtain more favorable terms than issuing in a single market. Bond placements by APEC developing countries reached a peak of $14 billion in the fourth quarter of 1993. Over the first half of 1994, new bond issues by these countries fell in response to overall developments in the market, but the share of APEC developing countries in total bonds issued internationally by developing countries rose.

Among APEC developing countries, Mexico has been the leading international bond issuer thus far in the 1990s (Appendix Table 5). Private firms accounted for the largest share of these issues, with the number of firms issuing and the size of issues expanding sharply in 1992 and 1993. Public sector corporations have also been major issuers, running only slightly behind private sector issues. Following a large issue in 1991, Mexican issues of sovereign bonds have declined in size and relative importance. Chile has not extensively tapped the international bond market since its return in 1991 with a sovereign issue. Another relatively small sovereign issue was placed in 1992, but, subsequently, only private Chilean firms have placed small issues internationally.

Hong Kong and Korea have been major issuers of bonds during the 1990s, placing the bulk of these issues in 1993. Bond placements by Hong Kong entities were entirely by private firms, while in the case of Korea, public sector entities accounted for a larger share than the private sector of the bonds placed. The private sector in Taiwan Province of China also placed substantial issues of new bonds in the first half of 1994.

The non-NIE Asian developing countries of APEC have also had a strong presence in the international bond markets in recent years, reflecting the return to the market of some of the major countries in this group after several years' absence. Each of these countries returned to the market through an issue by a major

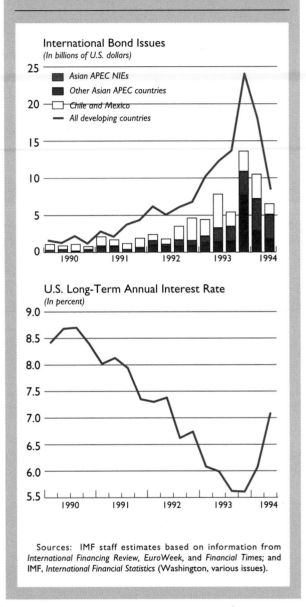

Chart 2-7. International Bond Issues by APEC Developing Countries and U.S. Long-Term Interest Rates, 1990–Second Quarter 1994

International Bond Issues
(In billions of U.S. dollars)

■ Asian APEC NIEs
■ Other Asian APEC countries
□ Chile and Mexico
— All developing countries

U.S. Long-Term Annual Interest Rate
(In percent)

Sources: IMF staff estimates based on information from *International Financing Review*, *EuroWeek*, and *Financial Times*; and IMF, *International Financial Statistics* (Washington, various issues).

public sector entity. China returned to international capital markets after a three-year absence with a Samurai bond issued by the China International Trust and Investment Corporation (CITIC) in October 1991, followed by additional large issues by public sector entities in 1992 and 1993.[5] After a six-year absence, the

---

[5] A Samurai bond is a yen-denominated bond issued in Japan by a foreign borrower. For public placements, issuers are required to have an investment-grade credit rating.

Government of China also re-entered the market with three bond issues in 1993. The Philippines regained access to the international bond markets for the first time since the debt crisis of the 1980s, when the Government placed a bond issue in February 1993; other public sector entities and private firms were also able to gain access to the market during 1993. Malaysia's return to the bond market in June 1993, after a four-year absence, was led by the state-owned petroleum company (Petronas). Private firms in Indonesia and Thailand were particularly large bond issuers in 1993 and in the first half of 1994.

Much of the borrowing by APEC developing countries through bonds so far has represented net capital inflows. Maturing bonds issued by these countries amounted to only $3 billion in 1990–93, compared with bond issues of $54 billion. As of the end of June 1994, the outstanding stock of international bonds issued by APEC developing countries was estimated to be $63 billion (about 53 percent of the total outstanding stock of international bonds issued by developing countries as a whole), with Asian members accounting for roughly 56 percent of the total APEC stock of bonds. Amortization payments on bonds issued by APEC developing countries are projected to rise significantly over the next few years, from about $2 billion in 1994 to a peak of $13 billion in 1998, as bullet repayments on bonds placed in the early 1990s fall due (Chart 2-8).[6] Mexico, in particular, has large amounts of bonds maturing during this period.

The terms of new issues by APEC developing countries have improved significantly during the 1990s. The average yield spread at launch declined from 397 basis points in 1990 to 129 basis points in the first quarter of 1994, with the most notable improvement achieved by private sector issuers (Appendix Table 6).[7] In the second quarter of 1994, unsettled conditions in the markets caused spreads to widen. Secondary market spreads for APEC developing country bonds generally followed a similar pattern. Terms on new issues by APEC developing countries have been better overall than those on bonds issued by other developing countries, with this difference being more pronounced for private sector borrowers than for public sector borrowers. During 1992–93, the average yield spread at launch for bonds issued by APEC developing countries was some 70 basis points lower than the corresponding

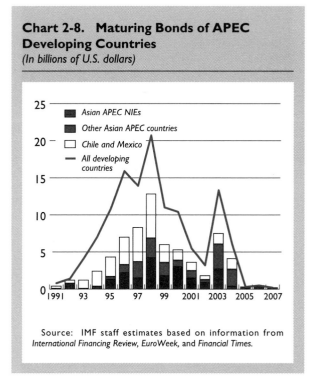

Chart 2-8. Maturing Bonds of APEC Developing Countries
(In billions of U.S. dollars)

Legend:
- Asian APEC NIEs
- Other Asian APEC countries
- Chile and Mexico
- All developing countries

Source: IMF staff estimates based on information from *International Financing Review*, *EuroWeek*, and *Financial Times*.

average for all developing countries; this difference was about 90 basis points for private sector issuers.[8] Within APEC developing countries, the Asian NIEs and other Asian countries, with the exception of the Philippines, commanded relatively low spreads, averaging 94 basis points and 135 basis points, respectively, in 1993. Chile and Mexico, both of which had experienced debt-servicing difficulties during the 1980s, paid higher spreads. Spreads at issue for Chilean bonds averaged less than 200 basis points. For Mexico, spreads have narrowed appreciably during the 1990s, falling from more than 350 basis points for public sector borrowers (more than 600 basis points for private sector borrowers) in 1990 to less than 200 basis points (around 350 basis points for private entities) in 1993.

The relatively favorable terms for APEC developing countries reflected the high credit ratings that have generally been assigned to them by major rating agencies. With the exception of Brunei and Papua New Guinea, all APEC developing countries have been assigned credit ratings; all rated countries, except Mexico and the Philippines, have received investment-grade ratings (Table 2-3).[9] Outside of APEC, only a

---

[6]These estimates may vary somewhat depending on whether market conditions evolve such that bondholders decide to exercise early redemption options on some bonds.

[7]In this section, spreads refer to the difference between the yield on a bond of a developing country entity and the yield on an industrial country government bond denominated in the same currency and of comparable maturity. Yields on U.S. treasury securities and comparable securities of other major industrial country governments are used as proxies for a risk-free return. Spreads are calculated only for bonds that do not include enhancements in their terms.

[8]These comparisons must be made carefully because the differences in yield spreads may reflect differences in the size of issues and their maturities, as well as differences in the credit quality of the issuers.

[9]Mexico has been assigned an investment-grade rating by one small U.S. agency, while the larger U.S. agencies have indicated periodically that consideration is being given to upgrading Mexico to investment grade.

Table 2-3. Credit Ratings of APEC Developing Country Sovereign Borrowers[1]

	Moody's Rating	S&P Rating	Recent Changes
Singapore	Aa2	AA+	Moody's upgraded rating from Aa3 in May 1994.
Taiwan Province of China	Aa3	AA+	Moody's assigned an Aa3 rating in March 1994.
Korea	A1	A+	
Thailand	A2	A–	
Malaysia	A2	A	Moody's upgraded rating from A3 in March 1993.
Hong Kong	A3	A	
China	A3	BBB	S&P assigned its BBB rating in February 1992, while Moody's assigned its rating A3 in September 1993.
Chile	Baa2	BBB+	Moody's assigned a Baa2 first-time investment rating in February 1994. S&P upgraded from BBB in December 1993.
Indonesia	Baa3	BBB–	S&P assigned first-time rating in July 1992.
Mexico	Ba2	BB+	S&P assigned first-time rating in July 1992.
(Par and discount bonds)	Ba3	BB+	
Philippines	Ba3	BB–	First-time ratings assigned in July 1993.

Sources: *Financial Times; International Financing Review;* and Salomon Brothers.
[1]Ranked in descending order according to rating. Ratings by Moody's Investor Service and Standard and Poor's. The ratings are ranked from highest to lowest as follows:

	Moody's	S&P
Investment grade	Aaa, Aa, A, Baa	AAA, AA+, AA, AA–, A+, A, A–, BBB+, BBB, BBB–
Noninvestment grade	Ba, B	BB+, BB, BB–, B+, B, B–
Default grade	Caa, Ca, C, D	CCC+, CCC, CCC–, CC, C

In addition, numbers from 1 (highest) to 3 are often attached to differentiate borrowers within a given grade.

few developing countries have achieved an investment-grade rating from a major rating agency.

APEC developing countries have tended to issue bonds that include enhancement techniques (for example., early redemption (put) options or equity conversions),[10] with a view to narrowing yield spreads at launch. Overall, 32 percent of total bond issues by APEC developing countries from 1990 through the first half of 1994 carried some form of enhancement (Appendix Table 7). In comparison, only 27 percent of all developing country bond issues carried enhancements during the same period. The pattern of enhancements has differed across countries and over time. During the early stages of regaining access to international financial markets, Mexican bond issues tended to feature the securitization of some type of revenue flow, such as export receipts, credit card receivables, and long distance telephone receipts. As Mexican entities established track records for timely payments on their bonds, this form of enhancement became less com-

mon. Issuers in Asian APEC developing countries have tended to use equity conversions and to a lesser extent put options. There was a noticeable shift to equity convertible options during the stock market booms in these countries. In the first half of 1994, turbulent market conditions led APEC developing countries to increase the use of techniques to enhance credit, particularly equity conversions and put options, with bonds carrying enhancements accounting for 59 percent of total issues.

Most bonds issued by APEC developing countries continue to be denominated in U.S. dollars because of the dominant size of this sector of the market and the strong interest of U.S. investors in the securities of these countries (Appendix Table 8). Yen-denominated bonds have accounted for a relatively small and slightly declining portion of total bond issues. Among the APEC developing countries, China has been the most active issuer of yen-denominated bonds, reflecting the considerable interest of Japanese investors in China.

In line with the experience of other developing countries, the majority of bond issues from the developing countries of APEC have been concentrated in the Eurobond market or through private placements, owing in part to less stringent disclosure standards. Mexican entities have issued the largest number of bonds out-

___
[10]A bond with a put option grants the bondholder the right to sell the bond back to the issuer at par on a designated date. A convertible bond contains a provision that grants the bondholder the right to convert the bond to a predetermined number of shares of common stock in the issuing company.

side the Euromarket, placing most of these issues in European currencies in local markets and some in the Samurai and Yankee markets. Borrowers in several Asian APEC developing countries, including China, Korea, and Malaysia, have also tapped the Samurai bond market. China, Indonesia, and Thailand have issued in the Yankee bond market as well.[11] A few APEC developing country issuers, including China and Mexico, have also made placements in the Dragon bond market.[12]

In recent years, international investors have shown increasing interest in purchasing financial instruments denominated in local currency in domestic markets. Interest has been particularly strong in some of the Asian APEC members (such as Indonesia and the Philippines) and in Mexico. Because exchange rates in these countries are relatively stable, sizable differentials between domestic and international interest rates have attracted large capital inflows. Reliable data on these flows, however, are not available.[13] Some indication of their potential magnitude is provided by the experience of Mexico, where foreign investors have been active purchasers of Mexican government treasury bills (*Cetes* and *Tesobonos*) and longer-term government paper (*Ajustabonos*). It is estimated that such investors now hold about 70 percent of outstanding *Cetes* and 55 percent of *Ajustabonos*.

Equities

Equity placements by APEC developing countries in international capital markets during the 1990s have been substantially smaller than bond issues but have nonetheless risen and represent a significant source of funding. These placements have grown steadily from $1.1 billion in 1990 to $8.1 billion in 1993 (Chart 2-9 and Appendix Table 9). As share prices in APEC developing countries fell sharply between February and April 1994, international equity placements by these countries declined from $4.5 billion in the final quarter of 1993 to $1.5 billion in the second quarter of 1994. Major equity issuers include China, Hong Kong, and Mexico, which together have accounted for 67 percent

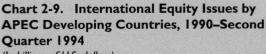

Chart 2-9. International Equity Issues by APEC Developing Countries, 1990–Second Quarter 1994
(In billions of U.S. dollars)

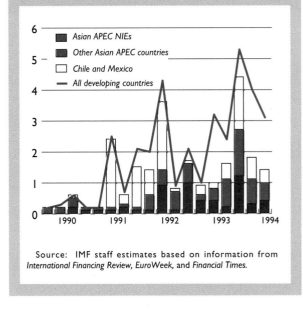

Source: IMF staff estimates based on information from *International Financing Review*, *EuroWeek*, and *Financial Times*.

of the total international stock issues by APEC developing countries during the period 1990 through the second quarter of 1994.

International equity placements have taken the form of American or global depository receipts (ADR/GDR) programs,[14] international tranches of new placements in domestic stock markets, and issues in foreign stock markets. Mexican companies have placed equity issues internationally almost exclusively through ADR/GDR programs. In contrast, Asian APEC developing countries have used international tranches of domestic stock issues and direct issues in foreign markets as their principal means of placing equities abroad (Appendix Table 10). China has been the major issuer among these countries. It has issued few equities through ADR/GDR programs, focusing instead on listing selected Chinese enterprises on the Hong Kong Stock Exchange (HKSE) (so-called H-shares). Between July 1993 and May 1994, nine Chinese companies had been listed on the HKSE, raising

---

[11]A Yankee bond is a U.S. dollar-denominated bond issued in the United States by a foreign borrower. Yankee issues are subject to U.S. Securities and Exchange Commission registration and disclosure requirements.

[12]A Dragon bond is a bond issued in the Asia-Pacific region outside of Japan in foreign currencies and listed on at least two securities exchanges in the region (mainly in Hong Kong, Singapore, and Taiwan Province of China).

[13]The World Bank is currently engaged in a project to develop an authoritative data base on portfolio capital flows directly into local bond and stock markets of developing countries by major recipient country. Among APEC members, Chile, Indonesia, Korea, Malaysia, Mexico, the Philippines, and Thailand are included in the project. Preliminary results of this study are expected to be available in early 1995.

---

[14]An ADR is a U.S. dollar-denominated equity-based instrument backed by shares in a foreign company held in trust. An ADR is traded like the underlying shares on major U.S. exchanges or in the over-the-counter market. The advantage of an ADR issue is that it allows companies in developing countries to broaden their investor base, while international investors can reduce their settlement and trading risks. A GDR is similar to an ADR but is issued and traded internationally.

about $1.5 billion, including a joint listing on the HKSE and the New York Stock Exchange (NYSE) for Shanghai Petrochemical Company.[15] Two Chinese firms have also been listed on the Singapore Stock Exchange.

Over the last few years, direct equity purchases by international investors on local exchanges have become an increasingly important source of portfolio flows to APEC developing countries. Although comprehensive statistics on these transactions are not available, partial information suggests that such purchases have increased significantly, for instance, more than doubling in Mexico, to an estimated $10.7 billion in 1993. Such purchases in 1993 are reported to have amounted to $4.3 billion for Korea, $2 billion for Indonesia, and $1.4 billion for the Philippines. In China, foreign investment in B-shares (shares that are traded on domestic exchanges with ownership restricted to foreigners) is estimated to be on the order of $2 billion in the period 1992–June 1994.

Emerging market mutual funds have played a major role in channeling portfolio flows to developing countries during the last few years. These mutual funds in general have focused on equities, with the number of equity funds and their net assets growing significantly. Equity funds specifically targeting APEC developing countries numbered 231 by the end of 1993, and their total net asset value amounted to $17 billion (Appendix Table 11).[16] It is estimated that net purchases of equities (including purchases of equities in international capital markets) through dedicated APEC developing country mutual funds averaged over $1 billion a year during 1990–93 (Appendix Table 12).[17] This estimate probably significantly understates the flow to APEC developing countries because Asian and Latin American regional funds and global funds are not included. These funds could be expected to make substantial investments in APEC developing country equities; however, these data are not available. In total, net equity flows from global and regional funds averaged about $2 billion and $3 billion a year, respectively, during 1990–93.

Sources and Destinations of Portfolio Capital Flows

Comprehensive data on sources of portfolio capital flows are unavailable, and only fragmentary information exists regarding the investor base in developing country securities overall.[18] Available information, however, gives a partial indication of the likely characteristics of investors in the securities of APEC developing countries.[19]

Investor Base

Asian countries that had maintained access to international markets continue to attract investments from mainstream institutional investors, especially in the United Kingdom and the United States. In contrast, Latin American countries probably experienced a significant reflow of flight capital as they begin to regain market access at the beginning of the 1990s. As noted above, the number of mutual funds dedicated to investing in developing country securities has also risen sharply. In 1992, the expansion in the investor base began to gain considerable momentum. Dedicated emerging market mutual funds continued to grow rapidly in terms of number and net asset value, while other mutual funds also began to purchase developing country securities. Reports suggest that some U.S. pension funds began to diversify their portfolios by holding these securities and that European institutional investors increased their holdings of these securities as well.

Investor preferences for developing country portfolio assets vary from country to country. U.S. investors play a major role in the market, largely focusing their purchases of debt and equity on issuers in Latin America and Asia. U.K. investors are also reported to be active in trading in developing country securities, tending to buy assets in Asia, and to a lesser extent, in Latin America. German investors are reported to be principally interested in issues by Eastern European countries but are beginning to show more interest in Latin American securities. Japanese investors have invested only a small share of their assets in develop-

---

[15]Previously, offshore special purpose entities affiliated with Chinese companies have been listed on the NYSE (e.g., Brilliance China Automobile, China Tire, and Ek Chor). Recently, additional Chinese firms have been listed on the NYSE.

[16]These funds usually hold about 10 percent of their portfolio in cash or other liquid industrial country assets. However, the data presented here may underestimate total mutual fund holdings of developing country assets because only those mutual funds that have invested more than 60 percent of their portfolio in emerging markets are included.

[17]An approximation for net purchases of APEC developing country equities by emerging market mutual funds can be obtained by adjusting the change in the funds' net assets for share price increases.

[18]Work is currently being done by the IMF Committee on Balance of Payments Statistics to improve data on portfolio capital flows. A coordinated survey of portfolio investment data for 1997 will be conducted to provide additional information on the geographic distribution of industrial countries' holdings of foreign securities and possibly information on other attributes of portfolio capital flows, such as their sources and destinations. It is hoped that, among APEC members, Australia, Canada, Japan, and the United States will participate in the study.

[19]A discussion of the investor base for developing country securities can be found in *International Capital Markets: Developments, Prospects, and Policy Issues*, World Economic and Financial Surveys (Washington: International Monetary Fund, 1994).

ing country portfolio issues, mainly in the issues of Asian countries.

Recipients of Flows

Data on international bond and equity placements offer some indication of the major sectors of the economies of the APEC developing countries that have been the prime recipients of portfolio capital flows. Financial institutions have been the major issuers of international bonds in these countries. From 1990 through June 1994, financial institutions raised $28 billion, 40 percent of total international bond issues by APEC developing countries; commercial banks alone accounted for 33 percent of total issues (Appendix Table 13). The financial sector's share was particularly high in China, Indonesia, Korea, Mexico, and Thailand. In China, financial institutions (including CITIC and the Bank of China) have, by government policy, acted as intermediaries (so-called windows) by borrowing abroad and then on-lending to domestic borrowers. In general, heavy international bond financing by financial institutions may raise important questions as to the capacity of the financial sector in a developing country to intermediate capital flows effectively and efficiently.[20]

In other sectors of APEC developing countries' economies, nonsovereign borrowers that have successfully placed issues in international markets have tended to be well-established entities with large domestic market shares or strong export potential. From 1990 through June 1994, firms in the petroleum industry were large issuers in Malaysia and Mexico. Utilities accounted for a significant share of total bond placements by Korea, Malaysia, and the Philippines, and telecommunications companies accounted for a substantial share of issues by Chile and the Philippines. The electrical equipment and electronics industries were major bond issuers in Korea and Taiwan Province of China. The real estate sectors in Hong Kong and Thailand were very active in placing bonds abroad. Cement companies in Indonesia and Mexico and steel companies in Korea were important issuers. The broadest sectoral range of borrowers with access to international markets was achieved by Hong Kong, Korea, Mexico, and Thailand.

International equity placements by companies in APEC developing countries (Appendix Table 14) have been concentrated in telecommunications, banks and financial services, manufacturing, electronics, media, and steel. On an individual country basis, Mexican issuance has been dominated by the telecommunication sector (Telmex); in Hong Kong, by the financial

sector; in Korea, by the electronics and shipping industries; and in China, by manufacturing firms. Privatization has played an important role in attracting equity investment from abroad, including Mexico's Telmex ($1.9 billion), China Steel in Taiwan Province of China ($0.4 billion), and Singapore's Telecome ($0.4 billion).

Portfolio Capital Flows Among APEC Countries

U.S. treasury data on transactions in foreign securities and Japan's regional balance of payments statistics provide a partial picture of portfolio flows among APEC countries. According to U.S. treasury data, U.S. investors shifted from net sales (including transactions on local financial markets) of $3.5 billion of APEC developing country securities (stocks and bonds) in 1991 to net purchases of $8.5 billion in 1992 and $20.9 billion in 1993 (Appendix Tables 15 and 16). U.S. bond purchases were concentrated in Mexican issues; U.S. investors sold holdings of bonds issued by Asian APEC NIEs throughout the period. U.S. equity purchases were concentrated in the same countries, although sizable purchases of Mexican stocks also took place. The United States is estimated to have directly accounted for at least 43 percent of net portfolio flows to APEC developing countries in 1992 and 56 percent in 1993. These figures, however, probably understate U.S. purchases of these countries' securities. The U.S. data show that net purchases of foreign securities from the United Kingdom reached nearly $55 billion in 1993, after averaging $26 billion a year in 1991–92. Major Eurobond dealers and a number of emerging markets mutual funds are located in London. Thus, it is likely that the ultimate destination of some significant portion of these portfolio flows to the United Kingdom included some of the developing country members of APEC.

By contrast, Japanese investors' purchases of developing country securities have been relatively limited. Japan's regional balance of payments statistics indicate that there were only small portfolio capital outflows directly from Japan to Southeast Asian countries and China during 1990–93 (Appendix Table 17).[21] At the same time, investors from this region made substantial portfolio investments in Japan, particularly in 1991

---

[20]The capacity of a developing country's financial sector to intermediate capital flows is discussed in Section IV of this Occasional Paper.

[21]In Japan's balance of payments data, Southeast Asia covers a broader range of countries than the APEC members in the region. Included are non-APEC member countries such as the Islamic State of Afghanistan, Bangladesh, Bhutan, India, Macao, Maldives, Myanmar, Nepal, Pakistan, and Sri Lanka. Actual portfolio capital flows from Japan to APEC developing countries are probably higher than the balance of payments data suggest, since some flows are recorded as going to third-country intermediaries (such as the United Kingdom and the United States) instead of to the ultimate destinations of these flows. The balance of payments data also understate flows because they do not reflect foreign security purchases that are not made through securities companies in Japan.

during the boom in the Japanese stock market. These flows probably reflect transactions with financial centers such as Hong Kong and Singapore and with Taiwan Province of China.

Data on Samurai bond issuance draw a similar picture (Appendix Table 18). Samurai bonds are a principal means for developing countries to reach Japanese investors. While Samurai bond issuance by APEC developing countries has increased significantly in recent years, the total amount of bonds issued in 1990–93 was limited to about $4.4 billion (¥ 521 billion). China became the leading Samurai bond issuer among APEC developing countries in 1992–93. Of the other developing country members of APEC, only Hong Kong, Korea, Malaysia, and Mexico have placed bond issues in this market.

According to data from the Japan Securities Dealers Association (JSDA) on Japanese purchases of equities on local stock exchanges in Asian APEC developing countries, only minimal stock purchases were made during the period 1992 to August 1994, and total Japanese holdings of equities issued by entities in these countries are very small (Appendix Table 19). Japanese investors are permitted to buy or sell, through securities houses in Japan, foreign stocks listed on only those stock exchanges designated by the JSDA. The number of APEC developing country stock exchanges desig-

nated by the JSDA is currently nine, including Shanghai and Shenzhen, which were added in March–April 1994 (Appendix Table 20).[22] No company from a developing country has had its stock listed on the Tokyo Stock Exchange—the only stock exchange in Japan on which foreign companies can be listed.[23] Japanese investors have also invested in developing country equities through closed-end investment trusts listed on the Osaka Securities Exchange. At the end of August 1994, six trusts were listed, five of which were dedicated to APEC developing countries (Appendix Table 21); five more funds are expected to be established by the end of 1994, two of which are to be dedicated to Asian APEC developing countries. While the assets of existing funds targeting APEC developing countries have grown significantly within a short time, reflecting Japanese investors' growing interest in Asian emerging markets, their net assets amounted to only $1.7 billion as of August 1994.

---

[22]Among APEC developing countries with existing local stock markets, only Chile and Taiwan Province of China are not included on the JSDA designation list. Outside the APEC developing countries, only one developing country stock exchange, the Buenos Aires Stock Exchange, is on this list.

[23]The number of foreign stocks listed on the Tokyo Stock Exchange has declined. Currently, 97 foreign companies are listed, compared with 127 at the end of 1991.

III Macroeconomic Management in APEC Economies: The Response to Capital Inflows

Mohsin S. Khan and Carmen M. Reinhart

In recent years, there has been a surge of international capital flows to many Asian countries. During 1990–93, developing economies in Asia received a net capital inflow of $151 billion, more than double the amount recorded for the previous four years. For certain Asian countries, such as Malaysia and Thailand, these inflows have amounted to as much as 15 percent of GDP (Chart 3-1). These developments represent a major turning point from the previous decade, when, because of the debt crisis, little capital flowed to most developing countries. This change is not limited to only a few countries. The number of economies in Asia experiencing a surge in capital inflows has recently expanded; among the more recent recipients of capital inflows are India, Nepal, and Sri Lanka. Other regions, in particular, Latin America and the Middle East, have also been attracting large amounts of foreign capital. While issues pertaining to the management of international debt dominated the policy discussions of the 1980s, the design of effective economic policies for dealing with these capital inflows, and for ensuring their durability, has become a key economic policy issue in recent years.[24]

Capital inflows—or, more generally, access to international capital markets—are often regarded as central to the development process. The historical experience of many industrial countries has shown that external financing helped facilitate investment and growth. The recent Asian experience indicates a similar pattern, as the surge in capital inflows has been accompanied by sharp increases in investment in the recipient countries (with investment/GDP ratios rising anywhere in the range of 2–10 percent during the past five years) and an acceleration in economic growth (Bercuson and Koenig (1993)). At the same time, capital inflows, particularly of the magnitudes currently observed in many Asian and Latin American countries, may pose serious dilemmas for economic policy. Large capital inflows are often associated with a rapid expansion of money and credit, inflationary pressures, a real exchange rate appreciation, and a deterioration in the current account of the balance of payments. In addition, they tend to

have a substantial impact on the stock market, the real estate market, and the money market—an impact that may well threaten the stability of these markets and of the financial system as a whole. Furthermore, if the capital inflows are purely short term, these problems intensify as the probability of an abrupt and sudden reversal increases.

This section describes the current episode of capital inflows to several Asian economies, summarizing the principal facts, the impact of the inflows, and policy options.[25] The discussion also covers, when relevant, the similar experiences of Latin American countries, with an emphasis on the policy priorities that could ensure the persistence and sustainability of these flows, as far as possible. The analysis draws heavily on previous work by Calvo, Leiderman, and Reinhart (1993, 1994, and forthcoming, 1995), who used data for ten Latin American countries and eight Asian countries, as well as other recent studies undertaken in the IMF (Goldstein and Mussa (1993), International Monetary Fund (1992 and 1993), and Schadler and others (1993)). The first part of this section describes the main characteristics and macroeconomic consequences of capital inflows to the Asian region. The second part discusses the role of external factors in the present inflows episode, as well as the likely factors that will determine the sustainability of these capital inflows. Finally, the relative merits of various policy responses to the surge in capital inflows are discussed.

Capital Inflows

Capital inflows are defined as the increase in net international indebtedness of the private and the public sectors and are measured—albeit imprecisely—by the surplus in the capital account of the balance of payments. Therefore, except for errors and omissions, the capital account surplus equals the excess of expenditure over income (which, in turn, is equal to the gap between national investment and national saving) *plus* the change in official holdings of international

---

[24]This issue is addressed in some detail in Calvo, Leiderman, and Reinhart (1993 and 1994) and Schadler and others (1993).

[25]The discussion covers all Asian countries as well as selected ones that are members of APEC.

Chart 3-1. Balance on the Capital Account
(In percent of GDP)

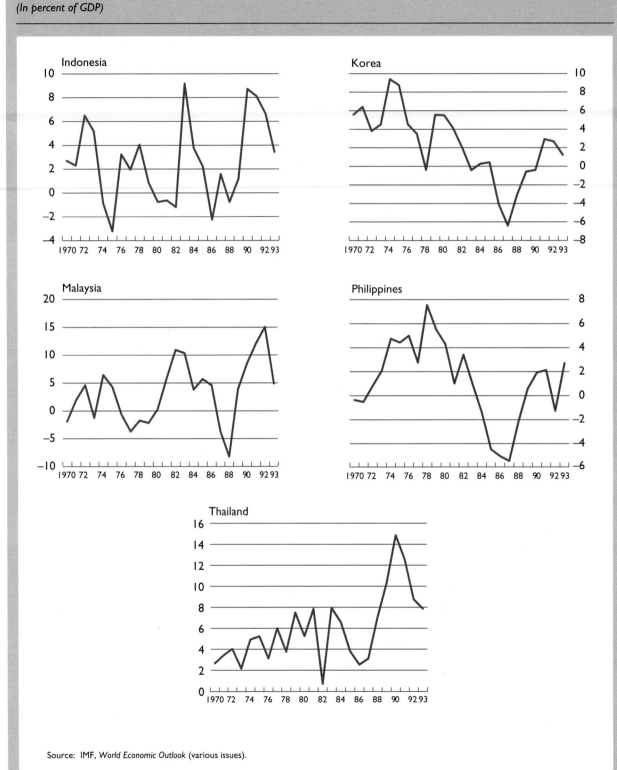

Source: IMF, *World Economic Outlook* (various issues).

Table 3-1. Asia: Balance of Payments
(In billions of U.S. dollars)

Year	Balance of Goods, Services, and Private Transfers[1]	Balance on Capital Account Plus Net Errors and Omissions[1]	Changes in Reserves[2]
1985	−16.6	19.5	−2.9
1986	0.9	22.7	−23.5
1987	17.9	23.3	−41.3
1988	5.7	5.9	−11.6
1989	−2.6	12.3	−9.6
1990	−5.8	29.2	−23.5
1991	−4.7	46.3	−41.5
1992	−8.2	30.1	−21.9
1993	−24.0	45.0	−21.0

Source: IMF, World Economic Outlook (various issues).

[1]A minus sign indicates a deficit in the pertinent account. The balance on goods, services, and private transfers is equal to the current account balance less official transfers. The latter are treated in this table as external financing and are included in the capital account.

[2]A minus sign indicates an increase.

reserves. Thus, increases in capital *inflows* can be identified with *larger* current account deficits and/or an *accumulation* of reserves.

The central bank of the recipient economy can react to increased capital inflows in various ways, depending mainly on the prevailing exchange rate regime. Under a pure float, the increased net exports of assets in the capital account finance an increase in net imports of goods and services. In this case, the authorities do not intervene in the foreign exchange market, and the inflows of capital from abroad are not associated with changes in central banks' holdings of official reserves. At the other extreme, the domestic authorities can actively intervene to maintain a fixed exchange rate. In the presence of a capital inflow, they would purchase the foreign exchange that flows in, and the increase in the capital account surplus would be associated with an increase in official reserves.

Characteristics of the Inflows

Capital began to flow to Thailand in 1988 and to a number of other Asian developing economies in 1989–90 (see Bercuson and Koenig (1993) and Chuhan, Claessens and Mamingi (1993)).[26] Table 3-1 presents a breakdown of Asia's balance of payments into its three

main accounts.[27] The capital inflows under consideration appear in the form of surpluses in the capital account of about $29 billion in 1990, about $46 billion in 1991, $30 billion in 1992, and $45 billion in 1993.

As far as composition is concerned, the capital that has flowed to developing countries in the 1990s is radically different from that of the earlier episodes, with commercial bank loans, which dominated the earlier periods, substantially replaced by foreign direct investment (FDI) and bond and equity portfolio flows (see Chart 3-2). It is evident from the data for Asia that an important part of the rise in capital inflows is due to marked increases in FDI, particularly in the early stages of the current episode (Table 3-2). It is well known that FDI is guided more by medium- or long-term profitability considerations than by portfolio investments and hence is probably subject to a smaller degree of sudden reversals than are portfolio flows. Moreover, FDI flows have positive externalities for the recipient economy, such as increased access to foreign markets and increased scope for human capital development and for introduction of top-of-the-line technology. Thus far, the investment flows have been directed mainly to service sectors such as transportation, telecommunications, and banking. Among the countries, FDI has been of greatest importance—relative to total capital inflows—in Malaysia and perhaps Thailand.[28]

[26]There are, however, important differences in the orders of magnitudes of the capital inflows among the five Asian countries considered. For instance, despite a substantial rise in 1992–93, capital inflows and investment have been lower in the Philippines than in its neighbors.

[27]The regional breakdown of developing countries corresponds to the classification used in the IMF's World Economic Outlook.

[28]Thailand's data on the composition of capital flows tend to understate foreign direct investment.

Chart 3-2. Capital Flows in Developing Countries
(In percent of total)

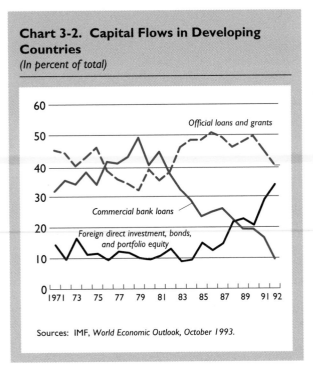

Sources: IMF, *World Economic Outlook*, October 1993.

Gooptu (1993)).[29] The growing demand for the equities and bonds of these countries by institutional and private investors in the United States, Japan, and other industrial countries has encouraged and facilitated a surge in bond and equity finance. As Table 3-3 shows, bond issuance nearly quadrupled between 1989 and 1992 and continued to soar during 1993. The trend in equity issuance is similar, although there are signs that the pace slowed somewhat for some countries during 1993. Direct equity portfolio purchases on local stock markets, especially by institutional investors, have become the most important channel for equity inflows into various emerging market economies and have fueled stock market booms (Chart 3-3). In recent years, total returns in Asian and other emerging stock markets have been considerably higher than in the United States and other industrial countries; during 1993, total stock market returns in U.S. dollars were 117 percent in Indonesia, 22 percent in Korea, 111 percent in Malaysia, 154 percent in the Philippines, and 114 percent in Thailand. International investors have clearly viewed Asia as fertile ground for raising their expected returns.

More recently, portfolio flows to countries in the region have risen dramatically almost across the board as bond and equity portfolios in many of the industrial countries have become more internationally diversified, gaining greater exposure to these countries (see

[29]For a few of the countries in the region, as well as for most Latin American countries, part of the surge in capital inflows is undoubtedly due to the repatriation of flight capital. In part, this return has been encouraged by a series of policy measures designed to reverse capital flight—such as amnesties, capital account liberalization, and introduction of domestic instruments denominated in foreign currency (see International Monetary Fund (1992) and Mathieson and Rojas-Suárez (1993)).

Table 3-2. Foreign Direct Investment for Selected Asian Countries
(In percent of GDP)

Year	Indonesia	Korea	Malaysia	Philippines	Thailand
1984	0.25	0.08	2.35	0.02	0.97
1985	0.35	0.21	1.92	−0.03	0.43
1986	0.37	0.31	2.43	0.47	0.53
1987	0.69	0.32	3.15	0.98	0.47
1988	0.71	0.41	3.25	2.59	1.47
1989	0.73	0.21	4.31	1.95	2.04
1990	1.17	−0.04	5.36	1.09	1.90
1991	1.29	−0.09	7.41	1.45	1.30
1992	1.35	−0.10	7.16	1.40	1.45
1993	1.21	−0.15	5.86	1.52	1.04

Source: IMF, *World Economic Outlook* (various issues).

Table 3-3. Bond and Equity Issues
(In millions of U.S. dollars)

	1989	1990	1991	1992	1993
International bond issues					
China	—	—	115	359	3,048
Hong Kong	193	66	100	185	657
Indonesia	175	80	369	493	485
Malaysia	425	—	—	—	954
Philippines	—	—	—	—	1,293
Singapore	—	105	—	—	—
Korea	258	1,105	2,012	3,208	5,864
Taiwan Province of China	100	—	160	60	79
Thailand	—	—	17	610	2,247
International equity issues					
China	—	—	11	1,049	1,908
Hong Kong	—	—	140	1,250	1,264
Indonesia	—	633	167	262	604
Korea	—	40	200	150	328
Malaysia	—	—	—	382	—
Philippines	—	53	159	392	64
Singapore	—	214	125	272	613
Taiwan Province of China	—	—	—	543	72
Thailand	—	100	209	145	466

Source: IMF staff estimates based on information from *International Financing Review* Equibase, *Euroweek*, and *Financial Times*.

A substantial proportion of the inflows has been channeled to reserves, which have increased by about $85 billion in the last four years. At the end of 1993, the stock of reserves for the Asian region stood at about $261 billion, well in excess of the combined stock of reserves of *all* developing countries (including economies in transition) outside the region. Overall, the sharp increase in official reserves indicates that in the face of the capital inflows, the monetary authorities in the region intervened quite heavily in the foreign exchange market to keep nominal exchange rates from appreciating significantly. Chart 3-4, which depicts monthly data on international reserves for a selected group of countries, confirms that all of the countries considered have experienced a pronounced upward trend in the stock of official reserves in recent years. However, the pace of accumulation of the reserves out of a given capital inflow is recently showing some signs of slowing (see Table 3-1). In part, this development may reflect the mounting opportunity costs associated with holding a large and rising stock of low-yield official foreign securities, particularly when interest rates on existing external and domestic debt are substantially higher. In part, the slower pace of reserve accumulation may also be due to the monetary authorities' greater willingness to accept a more appreciated nominal exchange rate as the inflows continue.

The rest of the capital inflows helped to finance a marked increase in the region's current account deficit—that is, an increased gap between national investment and national saving. As noted earlier, an important part of the inflows has financed increases in private investment. Since 1987, according to the *World Economic Outlook* (International Monetary Fund (various issues)), ratios of investment to GDP have risen by 6 percentage points in Korea, by 10 percentage points in Malaysia, by 5 percentage points in the Philippines, and by 7 percentage points in Thailand. The high and rising investment ratios, it is often noted, bode well for the growth prospects of the region and the countries' ability to service its debt.

Macroeconomic Effects

It is useful to compare the macroeconomic effects of capital inflows to Asia with the Latin American experience and focus on a broader set of countries. The main similarities between the two regions can be summarized as follows: First, as Table 3-4 illustrates, the swing in the balance on the capital account (as a percentage of GDP) is of a similar magnitude for the sample countries in the two regions. For the Latin American countries, the change in the capital account amounts to 4 percent of GDP; for the Asian countries, the capital account surplus increases by 2.7 percent of GDP. Second, as discussed, capital inflows in both regions have been associated with a marked accumulation of international reserves, indicating a heavy degree

Chart 3-3. Share Prices for Selected Emerging Markets in Asia
(IFC investable price indices in U.S. dollars; December 1988=100)

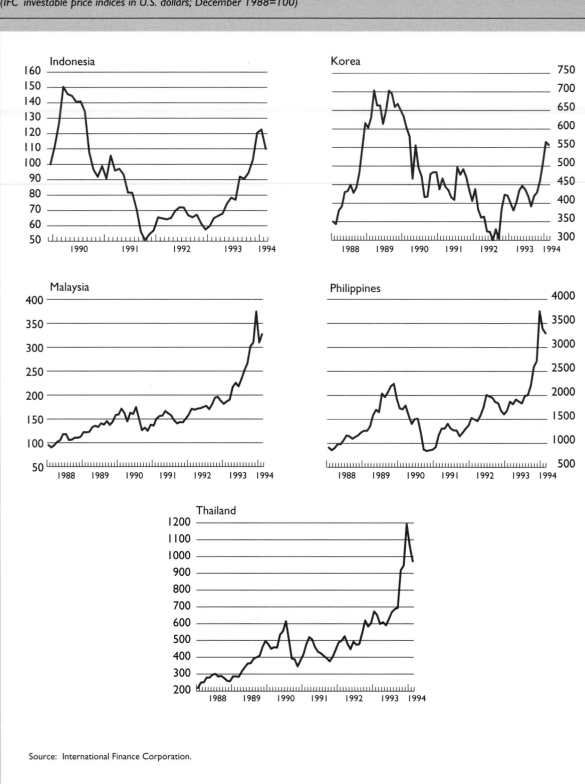

Source: International Finance Corporation.

Chart 3-4. Official Reserves for Selected Asian Countries
(In billions of U.S. dollars)

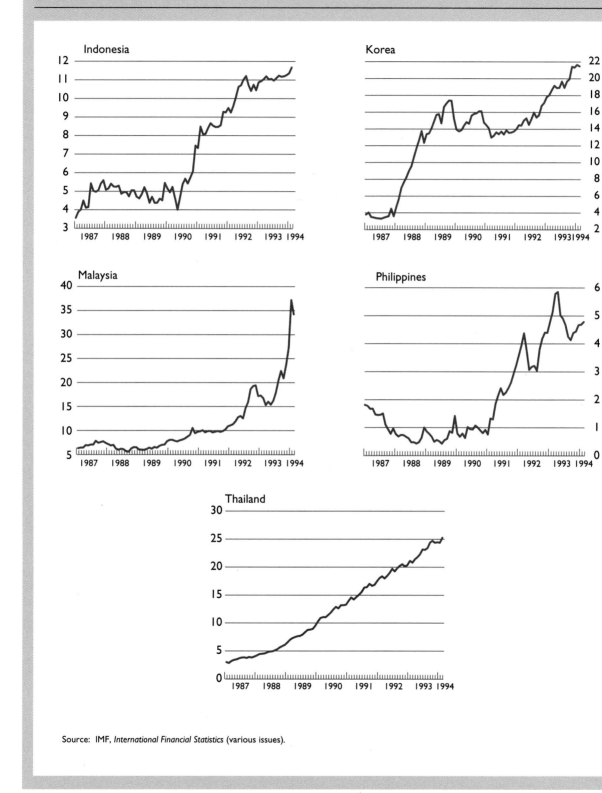

Source: IMF, *International Financial Statistics* (various issues).

Table 3-4. Key Indicators for Selected Latin American and Asian Economies
(In percent of GDP)

	Capital Account[1]		Direct Investment		Investment		Public Consumption	
	1984–89	1990–93	1984–89	1990–93	1984–89	1990–93	1984–89	1990–93
Latin America								
Argentina	−2.2	2.5	0.7	1.4	18.8	15.2	13.7	7.5
Bolivia	2.2	5.1	0.5	1.2	10.1	13.5	11.2	11.6
Brazil	−2.3	−0.4	0.5	0.2	17.1	15.3	11.1	12.1
Chile	−3.0	5.9	0.7	1.9	15.8	19.5	10.9	8.8
Colombia	1.7	0.7	1.5	1.5	16.0	14.6	9.2	10.1
Ecuador	−7.2	−3.7	0.5	1.4	19.2	18.8	11.6	7.8
Mexico	−0.4	6.1	0.8	1.6	16.8	20.6	11.5	10.3
Peru	−6.5	0.7	—	0.3	20.0	22.9	9.8	11.1
Uruguay	−2.9	−0.7	—	—	9.9	11.8	14.4	9.1
Venezuela	−2.9	−0.2	0.1	1.6	16.5	11.8	10.4	14.2
Average of ten countries	−2.4	1.6	0.5	1.1	16.0	16.4	11.4	10.2

	Capital Account		Direct Investment		Investment		Public Consumption	
	1984–88	1989–93	1984–88	1989–93	1984–88	1989–93	1984–88	1989–93
Asia								
Indonesia	0.9	6.7	0.5	1.1	24.3	27.8	10.0	10.0
Korea	−2.6	1.6	0.3	—	28.9	36.0	9.8	9.8
Malaysia	0.4	10.1	2.7	6.0	25.9	33.7	16.0	14.4
Philippines	−3.7	1.4	0.8	1.5	18.3	21.3	6.8	11.4
Singapore	8.1	−6.3	9.4	7.4	38.9	38.7	12.8	10.9
Sri Lanka	5.0	4.2	0.6	0.5	23.0	19.5	9.8	9.7
Taiwan Province of China	0.1	−3.5	−0.3	−1.5	19.3	23.5	15.0	16.1
Thailand	4.6	11.0	0.8	1.5	21.8	28.4	13.6	9.9
Average of eight countries	1.6	3.2	1.9	2.1	25.1	28.6	11.7	11.5

Source: IMF, *World Economic Outlook* (various issues), and *International Financial Statistics* (various issues).
[1]Includes errors and omissions.

of foreign exchange market intervention by the monetary authorities (Table 3-5). Third, the surge in capital inflows (particularly portfolio flows) has been accompanied by sharp increases in stock prices and, more generally, asset prices.[30] Share price indices in U.S. dollar terms for selected Latin American and Asian emerging markets were higher at the end of 1993 than at the time of renewal of capital inflows to these regions (Chart 3-3). Fourth, capital inflows have been accompanied by an acceleration in economic growth. Finally, reflecting in part the broad trend toward capital market liberalization and the greater sophistication of

domestic private enterprises, private bond and equity financing has played an increasingly important role.

But there are also important differences between the two regions. As discussed in Calvo, Leiderman, and Reinhart (1994 and forthcoming, 1995), in most Latin American countries capital inflows have been associated with considerable real exchange rate appreciation; yet as Chart 3-5 illustrates, in Asia such an appreciation is less common.[31] Although various reasons account for the variations in the response of the real exchange rate, important differences in the composi-

---

[30]Land prices have also posted strong increases in several countries; for a discussion of the case of Korea see Park and Park (forthcoming, 1995).

[31]For example, based on data from the IMF Information Notice System, the real exchange rates for Argentina, Mexico, and Uruguay appreciated by 169 percent, 35 percent, and 47 percent, respectively, during January 1990–October 1993. Of course, the appreciation of the real exchange rate can be a result of many factors.

Table 3-5. Latin America: Balance of Payments
(In billions of U.S. dollars)

Year	Balance of Goods, Services, and Private Transfers[1]	Balance of Capital Account Plus Net Errors and Omissions[1]	Changes in Reserves[2]
1985	−5.5	6.5	−1.0
1986	−19.9	12.9	7.0
1987	−12.9	16.2	−3.2
1988	−13.5	5.7	7.9
1989	−10.3	12.6	−2.3
1990	−7.7	23.3	−15.7
1991	−21.0	39.2	−18.2
1992	−36.3	59.4	−23.1
1993	−39.7	44.3	−4.5

Source: IMF, *World Economic Outlook* (various issues).

[1]A minus sign indicates a deficit in the pertinent account. Balance on goods, services, and private transfers is equal to the current account balance less official transfers. The latter are treated in this table as external financing and are included in the capital account.

[2]A minus sign indicates an increase.

tion of aggregate demand may play a key role in determining whether the real exchange rate appreciates or not. As Table 3-4 summarizes, for the Asian countries, investment as a share of GDP increased by about 3½ percentage points during the capital inflows period, but the investment ratio remained stagnant for the Latin American region. There are, however, marked differences among the Latin American countries. For example, both Chile and Mexico posted increases in investment during 1990–93. More recently, there are signs that investment has also been rising in Argentina, Colombia, and Peru. However, for the Latin American region, the inflows—particularly in 1990–91 during the initial stages of the surge—are primarily associated with a decline in private saving and higher consumption.[32] If the increased investment (in Asia) is tilted more toward imported capital goods and the increased consumption (in Latin America) has an imported domestic component, other things being equal, the real exchange rate appreciation in Latin America would tend to be stronger. In addition, differences in the domestic policy response are likely to play a key role in explaining the differences in real exchange rate behavior in the two regions. Specifically, the behavior of public sector consumption influences the real exchange rate by affecting both the level and composition of aggregate demand (Table 3-4). Other things being equal, the more restrained the fiscal stance at the

time of capital inflows, the weaker the real exchange rate appreciation. Although several Latin American countries (notably, Chile and Mexico) have had major fiscal adjustment programs, these predated the surge in capital inflows. By contrast, there were fiscal spending contractions in several Asian economies, most markedly in Thailand during 1988–91, at the time of the inflows (see Schadler and others (1993)). In addition, comparatively effective sterilization of capital inflows in Asia—which was successful in limiting the expansion in credit and money aggregates and in aggregate demand—may have contributed to the differences in real exchange rate behavior.

External Factors and Sustainability Issues

To determine the main causes of the resurgence of capital inflows to many developing countries in Asia and elsewhere, it is important to distinguish between the external and internal factors that gave rise to this development. External factors are those that are beyond the control of a given country and are thus unrelated to policies the country follows. Examples of such factors for small open economies are a decline in world interest rates and recession in the rest of the world, both of which may be accompanied by reduced profit opportunities in the industrial countries. A similar effect would arise from regulatory changes that provide incentives for further international diversification of investment portfolios at main financial centers. Some of these external factors are likely to have an important cyclical, or reversible, component. Internal

---

[32]Very disparate initial conditions in excess capacity between the two regions may help explain why investment surged in Asia and not in Latin America. Most Asian countries entered the capital inflow episode closer to full capacity utilization than their Latin American counterparts (an exception is Chile), where growth had been sluggish.

Chart 3-5. Real Exchange Rates for Selected Asian Countries

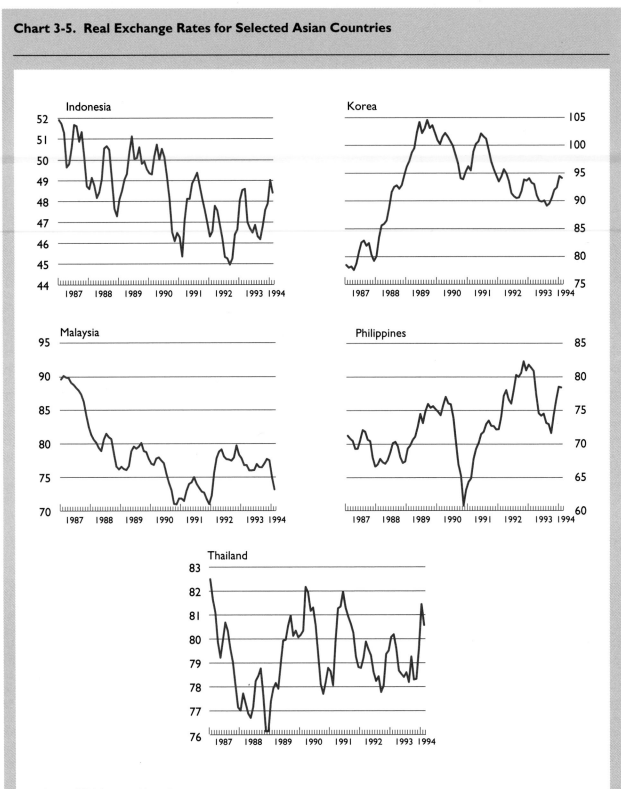

Source: IMF, Information Notice System.
Note: An increase in the index denotes a real exchange rate appreciation.

factors, on the other hand, are most often related to domestic policy. For example, countries can attract long-term capital inflows (possibly in the form of direct investment) by successfully implementing an inflation stabilization program; introducing major institutional reforms, such as the liberalization of the domestic capital market and the opening of the trade account; and instituting policies that result in credible increases in the rate of return on investment (such as tax credits). But domestic policies may also attract short-term, reversible capital, especially when these policies are not fully credible. Thus, partial credibility about inflation stabilization or trade liberalization programs can result in relatively high returns on short-term investments in view of the probability that these programs will collapse. Foreign investors could obtain relatively high profits under these circumstances if they managed to reverse their original inflows after they produced high yields and before the collapse of these policy programs.

Causes of the Inflows

Several events and underlying trends interacted in the late 1980s to make Asia potentially attractive for the renewal of capital inflows from abroad. First, there was a steep acceleration in the trends of institutionalization, globalization, and international diversification of investments in North America and other financial centers (see El-Erian (1992) for a discussion of key regulatory changes). This transformation is seen in the increasing amounts of funds being managed by mutual funds, pension funds, and life insurance companies. These entities began trying to raise expected returns and/or reduce overall risks by taking advantage of investments in emerging markets. Because the total assets of institutional investors are very large, even relatively small portfolio shifts that increase the weight attached to emerging markets can represent sizable capital inflows for the recipients.[33] In addition, regulatory changes in the United States have made it easier for foreign private issuers of equity to place their issues under conditions that are more attractive to investors. Second, several countries in Asia made significant progress toward improving relations with existing external creditors and reducing concerns about debt servicing. Third, and perhaps most important for long-term investment, several countries adopted sound monetary and fiscal policies, as well as market-oriented structural reforms that have included liberalizing trade, deregulating domestic financial markets, and eliminating capital account barriers. Fourth, and of the least importance to Asian countries, especially when compared with Latin America, repatriation of flight capital

facilitated the re-entry of capital to the region. Last, the relocation of labor-intensive industries from Japan, Korea, and Taiwan Province of China has played a key role in attracting capital flows to Southeast Asia (see Bercuson and Koenig (1993)). All these underlying factors helped re-establish credibility with foreign investors and provided the necessary conditions for the potential return of external capital to the region. Among the key external factors behind the current episode of capital inflows are the unusually low interest rates that have prevailed in the United States and Japan for the last four years. These low rates, combined with the persistent recessions in most industrial countries (which have also depressed returns in real estate and equity markets), have attracted investors to the high-investment yields and improving economic prospects of developing economies, such as those in Asia and Latin America. As shown by Fernandez-Arias (1993), low world interest rates have also improved creditworthiness indicators for various developing countries, especially those with considerable debt-service obligations.

For the Asian experience, Chuhan, Claessens, and Mamingi (1993) indicate that, while foreign influences played a significant role in stimulating bond and equity flows to several Asian countries, external developments were much less important than domestic ones in that region, accounting for about one-third of bond and equity flows to Asia. However, as the composition of capital inflows to Asia shifts more toward portfolio investment and proportionally less is accounted for by FDI, the sensitivity of flows to external financial variables may well increase.

Available empirical evidence for Latin American countries indicates that foreign developments have played a somewhat greater role in the most recent episode, accounting, according to Calvo, Leiderman, and Reinhart (1993), for 30–60 percent of the variance in real exchange rates and reserves. Similarly, Chuhan, Claessens, and Mamingi (1993) find that external factors explain about half of the bond and equity flows from the United States to a group of six Latin American countries.

The emphasis on external factors does not imply that domestic factors, such as structural reforms and stabilization, have played a negligible role. As discussed above, domestic policies have been essential for the re-entry of international capital. However, domestic factors alone cannot explain why capital inflows have also occurred in countries that have not undertaken reforms and have not stabilized, or why they did not occur in countries where reforms were introduced well before 1990.

Sustainability of the Capital Inflows

A critical question in most of the countries that experienced a surge in capital inflows is: To what

---

[33]For example, it is estimated that the assets of pension funds and life and casualty insurance companies reached $5.6 trillion in 1992.

extent will external and internal developments combine to make the flows endure? Part of the answer to this question depends on the continuation of underlying trends in the international financial system—that is, the globalization of markets and the diversification of investment portfolios. The growing interest of institutional investors in Asia (and other emerging markets) could continue throughout the rest of the 1990s in the form of a large portfolio shift. The movement of international capital into emerging markets has been based not only on high expected returns, but also on the idea that diversification can reduce overall risk in portfolios. The result is that Asian and Latin American securities are increasingly sold in the United States and other markets. Over time, individual countries have been able to rely less on returning flight capital and have achieved a broader investor base. Cementing these portfolio trends is a step in the direction of regional trade agreements.

Nevertheless, other factors work in the opposite direction. In particular, the prevailing global environment of low interest rates and weak activity in the industrial countries will change. As the global economy recovers, international interest rates may increase and capital market conditions may tighten. The tightening of monetary policy in the United States in February 1994 may be an early signal of that change. Furthermore, new competitors are likely to emerge as economic and political conditions in Eastern Europe and the former Soviet Union and other parts of the world improve. Such developments raise the possibility of reversals—especially in markets characterized by bubbles and in countries where the inflows are mostly short term.[34] In the face of heavy sales of domestic securities by foreign investors, the liquidity of financial markets in various countries would be put to a difficult test.

Sustainability and durability also depend on internal conditions. Sound macroeconomic policies, a strong commitment to market-oriented reforms, and outward-oriented trade strategies are likely to enhance the credibility of a country's policymakers from the standpoint of international investors. Economically, countries make the most efficient use of capital inflows if the investment return on these resources is higher than their cost. Policies that promote high domestic saving and adequate returns on domestic investment would be beneficial in this context. As noted earlier, in some countries, the financial intermediation of capital inflows is a source of concern. For the individual investor, the possibilities for hedging against these risks are limited in developing countries. Under these conditions, it is necessary to ensure adequate regulation and supervision of the banking system to avoid currency or term-structure mismatches and excessive credit creation, which could damage the ability of the financial system to deal with a reversal of capital flows.

Policy Response

The appropriate policy response to capital inflows clearly depends on the composition of the inflows (that is, whether they are short or long term), the availability and flexibility of various policy instruments, and the nature of domestic financial markets.[35] In addition, the prevailing policy environment and the extent of policymakers' credibility are key determinants of the form and timing of the appropriate policy response.

The rationale for policy intervention emerges from concerns that capital inflows can lead to inflationary pressures, real exchange rate appreciation and loss of competitiveness, and a deterioration of the current account. In addition, the inflows can destabilize domestic financial markets. These concerns have often led the authorities to react to the capital inflows by implementing a variety of policy measures. The role and relative merits of some of those policies are examined below.

Monetary and Exchange Rate Policy

Most of the recipient countries have implemented monetary and exchange rate policies in response to the shifting patterns of international capital flows. However, the policies have been quite varied.

Greater Exchange Rate Flexibility

A country that experiences a capital inflow may opt to let the nominal exchange rate appreciate. This option has three main virtues. First, it insulates the money supply, domestic credit, and more generally, the banking system from the inflows; this is particularly desirable if the inflows are perceived to be reversible. Second, because of a pass-through from the exchange rate to domestic prices, it may help reduce inflation—precisely at a time when achieving price stability is high on the policymakers' agenda. Third, allowing the exchange rate to fluctuate introduces uncertainty, which may well discourage some of the purely speculative (and highly reversible) inflows. The main disadvantage of a pure float is that massive capital inflows may induce a steep nominal *and* real appreciation of the domestic currency, which, in turn, may damage strategic sectors of the economy, like nontraditional

---

[34]Many emerging markets, including several in Asia, have witnessed historic highs in price-earnings ratios.

[35]Unfortunately, the policy choice is often complicated by data that do not reliably differentiate between short-term and long-term inflows.

exports. Damage would be inevitable if the real appreciation were to persist. But, even if the appreciation did not persist, the greater real exchange rate volatility could have negative effects on tradable goods sectors (see, for instance, Grobar (1993)) to the extent that financial markets do not provide enough instruments to hedge against such uncertainty.

There have been wide differences among countries in the degree of exchange rate flexibility in the present episode. However, the common ground appears to be that all central banks intervene in the foreign exchange market to some degree and that no country has operated under a free float. Among the Latin American countries, Chile and Mexico have allowed some degree of exchange rate flexibility in the context of their exchange rate bands. In Chile especially, the exchange rate has been allowed to fluctuate extensively within the band. (For various aspects of exchange rate bands in Chile and Mexico, see Helpman, Leiderman, and Bufman (1994)). Among the Asian countries, Korea intends to further widen the margins for daily exchange rate fluctuations, with the aim of moving toward a free float in two to three years.[36] Other countries, such as Colombia, Malaysia, Singapore, and Taiwan Province of China, have allowed for some appreciation of the nominal exchange rate. As indicated, one advantage of allowing nominal exchange rate appreciation is that to the extent that market fundamentals call for a real exchange rate appreciation, the latter can be effected all at once through the nominal appreciation of the exchange rate rather than gradually through increases in domestic inflation.

Sterilized Versus Nonsterilized Intervention

Once the decision is made to intervene in the foreign exchange market, the next policy question is whether intervention should be sterilized. Sterilization—the exchange of domestic securities for foreign exchange—can help attenuate the impact of capital inflows on money and credit. Sterilized intervention is essentially an attempt to insulate the domestic economy from the macroeconomic effects of capital inflows. Curtailing the growth of the monetary aggregates may be desirable for a variety of reasons: as the availability of credit increases, the quality of the loans made may well decline, placing the banking system at higher risk; a too-rapid expansion may cause the economy to "overheat" and fuel inflationary pressures; if the monetary authorities have announced monetary targets, growth in excess of those targets may damage their credibility. However, at a minimum, sterilized intervention will keep domestic interest rates higher than they would

have been in the absence of sterilization. At worst, this measure may well raise domestic interest rates and provide incentives for further short-term inflows—as occurred in Colombia in 1991 and Malaysia in 1991–92. In addition, sterilization results in an increase in the public debt and entails quasi-fiscal costs to the extent that the interest rate on domestic bonds is higher than that on foreign exchange reserves. Estimates of these costs in Latin American countries range from 0.25 percent to 0.50 percent of GDP a year (Kiguel and Leiderman (1993)). The cross-country evidence reveals that sterilized intervention (in varying orders of magnitude) has been the most common policy response to capital inflows in both Asia and Latin America.

Nonsterilized intervention may be desirable if the demand for money is perceived to increase owing, for example, to a successful inflation stabilization program that the authorities wish to accommodate. Under those circumstances, rapid monetary growth is not necessarily inflationary, and no quasi-fiscal burdens are generated. However, nonsterilized intervention, as noted, runs the risk of increasing the vulnerability of the financial system, especially if there is a system of explicit or implicit deposit insurance and banking supervision is poor. It is important to note that in many Asian countries the domestic banks are losing their "preferred" corporate clients, who are finding it more attractive to tap the international bond and equity markets directly. From an overall macroeconomic perspective, nonsterilized intervention is a more attractive option for a banking system with less capability or willingness to increase loans to the private sector, particularly for consumption purposes.[37] When the banking system is unable to intermediate more funds, additional capital inflows through the banking system will exert a strong downward pressure on interest rates, slowing the pace of inflows and lowering the fiscal cost of the outstanding domestic credit. However, most of the countries considered are not currently in this situation.

Reserve Requirements

A viable policy option that limits the expansion of money and credit associated with the surge in capital inflows is to increase bank reserve requirements and curtail access to rediscount facilities. This option would be especially relevant in those countries where capital inflows have taken the form of substantial increases in local bank accounts. Increasing marginal reserve requirements—an option exercised by Chile and Malaysia—clearly lowers banks' capacity to lend, thus diminishing some of the risks associated with

---

[36]During 1991–92, Korea's exchange rate policy was characterized by significant exchange rate intervention in response to capital inflows.

[37]Malaysia, for instance, has attempted to curb consumer credit by imposing restrictions on loans for purchases of motor vehicles and adopting stricter guidelines on the issuance of credit cards.

nonsterilized intervention without incurring quasi-fiscal costs. A drawback of this reserve requirement policy is that it is a onetime measure, and it may ultimately promote disintermediation, as new institutions may develop so as to bypass the regulations. Eventually, these institutions could grow until they are considered too large to fail and end up under the insurance umbrella of the central bank, re-creating all the potential problems associated with nonsterilized intervention. Therefore, increasing marginal reserve requirements is unlikely to be effective beyond the short run. Moreover, increasing bank reserve requirements amounts to a reversal of the underlying trend of financial liberalization that has been occurring in developing countries, under which these requirements have recently been sharply reduced toward the levels observed in industrial countries.

Banking Regulation and Supervision

A major concern about the intermediation of international capital flows through the domestic banking system is that individual banks are subject to free or subsidized deposit insurance. In other words, there is an implicit commitment by the authorities that banks—especially the large ones—will not be allowed to fail. It is well known that free implicit deposit insurance induces banks to increase their risk exposure. In several Latin American countries, there has been a sharp expansion of bank loans to finance private consumption. There is evidence that in some of these countries the percentage of nonperforming loans has recently increased over time. In addition, banks may pay little attention to matching the maturities of deposits against those for loans—the former being typically shorter than the latter. Similarly, there could be a mismatch between the currency denomination of bank loans and the currency denomination of profits and incomes of the borrowing sector, for example, if a producer of a nontradable good borrows in U.S. dollars. All these factors increase the vulnerability of the financial system to reversals in capital flows—reversals that have the potential to end in financial crisis.

Effective bank regulation and supervision can diminish some of these risks. As discussed earlier, attempting to insulate the banking system from short-term capital flows is a particularly important goal in cases where the inflows are predominantly in the form of short-term bank deposits. Regulations that limit banks' exposure to the volatility in equity and real estate markets could help insulate the banking system from the potential bubbles associated with sizable capital inflows. In this vein, risk-based capital requirements in conjunction with adequate banking supervision to ensure such requirements are complied with could help insulate the domestic banking system from the vagaries of capital flows.

Fiscal Policy

Some countries have complemented monetary and exchange rate policies with fiscal measures, such as the taxation of capital inflows and/or a reduction in public expenditure.

Taxing Short-Term Inflows

Taxes on short-term borrowing abroad were imposed in some countries—Israel in 1978 and Chile in 1991. This policy conveys the powerful message that the authorities are concerned with short-term, potentially speculative inflows. Such policies can coexist with policies that encourage a different type of inflow, specifically foreign direct investment. Unlike other measures, such taxes attack the problem at the source. However, although they can be effective in the short run, experience shows that the private sector is quick to find ways to circumvent the taxes through over- and underinvoicing of imports and exports and increased reliance on parallel financial and foreign exchange markets. Further, initial conditions are not always conducive to a policy that adds barriers to international capital movements. If a country has recently undertaken an adjustment program and the authorities enjoy less-than-full credibility, imposing a capital account barrier may be interpreted as signaling a policy reversal and may thus undermine the success of the program.

Fiscal Tightening

Another policy reaction to capital inflows has been to tighten fiscal policy; the clearest example of this policy is Thailand during 1988–91. The idea is to use fiscal restraint, especially in the form of spending cuts on nontradables, so as to lower aggregate demand and curb the inflationary impact of capital inflows.[38] Lower government expenditure on nontraded goods and services could have a direct impact on aggregate demand, which is unlikely to be offset by an expansion of private sector demand. However, contraction of government expenditure is always a sensitive political issue and cannot be undertaken on short notice. Delaying fiscal restraint, however, increases the risk that, ex post, the policy is procyclical. Moreover, fiscal policy is usually set on the basis of medium- or long-term considerations rather than in response to what may turn out to be short-term fluctuations in international capital flows. Thailand exemplifies this policy dilemma. The combination of booming growth and the substantive fiscal restraint of the past few years has generated a

---

[38]In addition, to the extent that it reduces the government's need to issue debt, a tighter fiscal stance is also likely to lower domestic interest rates.

perceived need to improve the current infrastructure, which is no longer adequate if rapid growth is to be sustained. At the same time, the pressures on the real exchange rate that accompany the surge in inflows would warrant fiscal restraint. However, in cases where the authorities had envisioned tightening the fiscal stance, a surge in capital inflows may call for earlier and, perhaps, more aggressive action.

Structural Measures

Various countries have adopted structural measures to indirectly or directly diminish the size, or the potential adverse effects, of capital inflows. Several of the Asian and Latin American countries have either undertaken or are considering undertaking capital account liberalization. For instance, in 1993 Thailand removed most of the controls on capital outflows, while Chile adopted similar, but more modest, measures in March 1994. These countries have followed the general principle that allowing domestic agents to hold foreign assets generates some offsetting capital outflow following the liberalization. However, the net impact of these measures on the capital account is not yet conclusive. In some cases, as the recent experience of Colombia highlights, the liberalization measures increased the confidence of foreign investors and, in so doing, further stimulated inflows.

In some cases, the presence of capital inflows and the stronger economic activity were used to implement trade liberalization and domestic financial reforms more rapidly. In principle, the surges in capital inflows present countries with a good opportunity to liberalize trade, which would tend to dampen the impact of the capital inflows on the exchange rate. Colombia, Indonesia, and Thailand are among the countries that undertook important steps toward liberalizing trade. While the trend is toward integrating goods and capital markets, some countries have experienced pressure to increase export subsidies to mitigate the effects of a sustained real exchange rate appreciation, a policy that is known to result in substantial fiscal costs and in deeper economic distortions. Overall, with regard to structural policies, it appears these should be designed so as to be consistent with longer-term objectives, rather than as a response to short-term capital inflows.

Policy Mix and Sequencing

The above discussion has highlighted that the risks associated with capital inflows create policy dilemmas. However, the overall picture is much more positive, as many Asian countries and a smaller number of Latin American countries have used these inflows to finance productive investment and achieve higher growth. There are no policy "tricks" for managing the inflows; the appropriate policy mix will depend on the nature of the inflows (in particular, their reversibility), their causes, and the macroeconomic and policy climate of the recipient country. To reduce the probability of a sudden reversal, policymakers must be able to maintain a high degree of credibility and be prepared to support clear market-oriented policies. Although no single policy recipe exists for all countries, to limit some of the risks associated with short-term flows, a reasonable sequencing of policies would consist in initially limiting the intermediation of those flows through sterilized intervention, greater exchange rate flexibility, and/or increased marginal reserve requirements, followed by a gradual monetization of these flows (that is, nonsterilized intervention), accompanied perhaps by an appreciation of the currency. The step to nonsterilized intervention can be speeded up if credit availability is limited and/or if the quasi-fiscal costs are high and if the implied creation of credit and money does not constitute a strong force toward an acceleration of inflation.

Last, it seems essential for countries to have flexible policy instruments that can respond quickly to adverse events, such as an abrupt reversal of capital flows. Holding an adequate level of reserves and allowing for some degree of exchange rate flexibility, possibly through an exchange rate band or similar mechanism, can work in this direction.

References

Bercuson, Kenneth B., and Linda M. Koenig, *The Recent Surge in Capital Inflows to Three ASEAN Countries: Causes and Macroeconomic Impact,* Occasional Paper No. 15 (Kuala Lumpur, Malaysia: South East Asian Central Banks, 1993).

Calvo, Guillermo, Leonardo Leiderman, and Carmen Reinhart, "Capital Inflows and Real Exchange Rate Appreciation in Latin America: The Role of External Factors," *Staff Papers,* International Monetary Fund, Vol. 40 (March 1993), pp. 108–51.

———, "The Capital Inflows Problem: Concepts and Issues," *Contemporary Economic Policy,* Vol. 12 (1994), pp. 54–66.

———, "Capital Inflows to Latin America: With a Reference to the Asian Experience," in *Capital Controls, Exchange Rates and Monetary Policy in the World Economy,* edited by S. Edwards (forthcoming, Cambridge: Cambridge University Press, 1995).

Chuhan, Punam, Stijn Claessens, and Nlandu Mamingi, "Equity and Bond Flows to Latin America and Asia: The Role of Global and Country Factors" (unpublished; Washington: World Bank, June 1993).

El-Erian, Mohamed A., "Restoration of Access to Voluntary Capital Market Financing," *Staff Papers,* International Monetary Fund, Vol. 39 (March 1992), pp. 175–94.

Fernandez-Arias, Eduardo, "The New Wave of Private Capital Inflows: Push or Pull?" (unpublished; Washington: World Bank, November 1993).

Goldstein, Morris, and Michael Mussa, "The Integration of World Capital Markets," IMF Working Paper 93/95 (Washington: International Fund, December 1993).

Gooptu, Sudarshan, "Portfolio Investment Flows to Emerging Markets," in *Portfolio Investment in Developing Countries*, edited by S. Claessens and S. Gooptu (Washington: World Bank, 1993).

Grobar, Lisa M., "The Effect of Real Exchange Rate Uncertainty on LDC Manufactured Exports," *Journal of Development Economics*, Vol. 41 (August 1993), pp. 367–76.

Helpman, Elhanan, Leonardo Leiderman, and Gil Bufman, "A New Breed of Exchange Rate Bands: Chile, Israel, and Mexico," *Economic Policy*: A European Forum, Vol. 9 (October 1994), pp. 260–306.

International Monetary Fund, *Determinants and Systemic Consequences of International Capital Flows*, IMF Occasional Paper No. 77 (Washington: International Monetary Fund, March 1991).

_____, *Private Market Financing for Developing Countries*, World Economic and Financial Survey Series (Washington: International Monetary Fund, 1992 and 1993).

_____, *International Financial Statistics* (Washington: International Monetary Fund, various issues).

_____, *World Economic Outlook* (Washington: International Monetary Fund, various issues).

Kiguel, Miguel, and Leonardo Leiderman, "On the Consequences of Sterilized Intervention in Latin America: The Cases of Colombia and Chile" (unpublished; Washington: World Bank, 1993).

Mathieson, Donald J., and Liliana Rojas-Suárez, *Liberalization of the Capital Account: Experiences and Issues*, IMF Occasional Paper No. 103 (Washington: International Monetary Fund, 1993).

Park, Y.C., and W. Park, "Capital Movement, Real Asset Speculation, and Macroeconomic Adjustment in Korea," in *Capital Controls, Exchange Rates and Monetary Policy in the World Economy*, edited by S. Edwards (forthcoming, Cambridge: Cambridge University Press, 1995).

Reisen, Helmut, "Southeast Asia and the 'Impossible Trinity,'" *International Economic Insights*, Vol. 4 (May–June 1993), pp. 21–23.

Schadler, Susan, Maria Carkovic, Adam Bennett, and Robert Kahn, *Recent Experiences with Surges in Capital Inflows,* IMF Occasional Paper No. 108 (Washington: International Monetary Fund, 1993).

IV Effect of Capital Flows on the Domestic Financial Sectors in APEC Developing Countries

David Folkerts-Landau, Garry J. Schinasi, Marcel Cassard, Victor K. Ng, Carmen M. Reinhart, and Michael G. Spencer

Studies of recent episodes of major capital inflows into APEC developing countries have focused almost exclusively on the macroeconomic implications of the flows, including their macroeconomic causes and effects and the appropriate policy responses.[39] The impact of the surge in capital flows on real exchange rates, trade flows, domestic investment, international reserves, and economic activity has been documented for many of the APEC developing countries and for many other developing countries. In addition, the effectiveness and relative merits of various policy measures—including monetary, exchange rate, and fiscal policies—in dealing with the surge in inflows have also been examined in light of recent country experiences. In particular, experience and existing studies suggest that sterilization to offset the monetary impact of capital inflows is likely to be effective only in the short run. Monetary expansions induced by capital inflows can be effectively curtailed through a nominal exchange rate appreciation and, if real exchange rate appreciation is a concern, through reduction in public spending (see Calvo, Liederman, and Reinhart (1993) and Schadler and others (1993)). The taxation of short-term capital inflows might be effective in the short run, but its effectiveness erodes over time.

However, the large volume of capital inflows has raised a number of other important issues. What are the effects of capital inflows on banking systems and capital markets in recipient countries? Have financial risks in recipient countries increased as a result of the changes in balance sheets and asset-price volatility brought about by rapid changes in the volume and composition of capital inflows? Is the existing financial infrastructure—including regulatory, supervisory, and accounting arrangements—capable of fostering an adequate management of these risks?

The need to ensure that these issues are given adequate attention can hardly be overstated. As a group, the developing countries are expected to require more than $1 trillion of domestic and foreign capital by the year 2000 to build the physical infrastructure necessary to sustain desired growth rates (World Bank (1994)). In 1993, net medium- and long-term capital inflows to the APEC developing countries amounted to almost $90 billion, or about 85 percent of total net capital inflows to all developing countries. The ability of the APEC developing countries to attract and effectively intermediate such a volume of financial flows depends importantly on the comprehensiveness, independence, and enforceability of the regulatory and supervisory frameworks in these financial systems. These frameworks need to ensure (1) that banking systems, which are going to remain the main conduit for the flows of funds into the countries, allocate credit efficiently in an environment where balance sheets are expanding as a result of capital inflows; and (2) that the stability of domestic capital markets is not adversely affected by cross-border flows and that capital markets possess sufficient integrity and transparency to retain investor confidence.

In the APEC developing countries, where banking institutions have retained a predominant role as financial intermediaries, a significant portion of these capital inflows either entered the recipient countries directly through, or ultimately were deposited in, the banking system of the recipient country. As a result, capital inflows have led to an expansion of bank balance sheets in several of these countries. It is therefore important to ensure that the regulation and supervision of banks are strong enough to ensure that credit quality does not deteriorate. The occurrence of costly financial crises in the recent past in some APEC developing countries has shown that concerns about the ability of these countries to maintain credit quality are not without foundation.[40]

---

[39]For an analysis of these issues for several APEC countries see Section II, and Bercuson and Koenig (1993).

[40]Several APEC developing countries are currently experiencing financial sector problems. In Malaysia, nonperforming loans rose sharply after the onset of recession in 1985 and peaked at 32 percent of total bank loans in 1988; this ratio fell to 12 percent at end-1993. In Indonesia, nonperforming loans held by commercial banks increased significantly in the early 1990s, reaching 16 percent of outstanding loans; this ratio fell from 14 percent in June 1993 to 5 percent in March 1994, in part the result of a reduction in the value of loans at problem banks and because of growth in new loans. Nonperforming loans in Korea amounted to 6 percent of total bank loans in mid-1993, and in Mexico, nonperforming assets rose from 2 percent of bank loans in 1991 to 6 percent in September 1993. These asset quality data compare unfavorably to the asset quality in several

In addition, international capital markets have changed dramatically during the past decade, and these changes have presented serious challenges for the countries that are recipients of international capital flows. In particular, the internationalization of institutional funds management—made possible by a continuing liberalization of cross-border flows—has generated a significant supply of yield-sensitive flows that tend to be highly responsive to changes in sentiment about the economic prospects of recipient countries. Indeed, the distinction between long-term international portfolio investment and short-term "hot money" is no longer helpful. Much of international portfolio investment is driven by transactions rather than taking the form of long-term expectations on the economic success of the recipient countries. It is therefore important that financial systems have not only a robust market infrastructure—wholesale payments, securities settlement, and clearance systems—but also financially resilient intermediaries that can cope with sudden reversals of financial flows and with volatile asset prices.

The APEC developing countries face the policy challenge of building a supervisory and regulatory infrastructure that (1) ensures the efficient allocation of bank credit, and (2) safeguards the integrity and stability of capital markets. Although many of these countries have made great strides in liberalizing and strengthening their financial systems in recent years, much remains to be done.

Banking Sector as a Conduit for Capital Inflows

In the APEC developing countries, banking institutions retain a predominant role as financial intermediaries, with bank assets accounting for at least 60 percent of total financial assets in most countries. Capital inflows either flow directly through the banking sector or affect the banking sector indirectly. Because of the predominance of banks, the soundness of the banking sector and the integrity of bank credit decisions are key components in the management of capital inflows. In many countries, and under varying circumstances, banking problems have most often been the result of bad credit decisions and inept management of credit risk, including overexposure to certain types of risk, and have caused major losses. Large and relatively volatile capital flows can contribute to these problems, especially when bank balance sheets are badly structured, by causing large swings in bank liquidity that result in alternating periods of credit expansion and contraction.[41] Two major areas of concern are the ability of the banking system to assess, price, and manage risk, and the adequacy of the supervisory and regulatory frameworks to prevent and contain systemic risk, particularly in the presence of safety nets and the problem of moral hazard. These elements of the financial system—intermediation, the assessment, pricing, and management of private risk, and the management of systemic risk—clearly influence the ability of policymakers to achieve economic objectives and are likely to play a primary role in allocating the capital inflows that will clearly be necessary for sustained economic growth.

An important recent concern in many developing countries that have undertaken financial liberalization is whether their relatively immature financial systems are capable of operating effectively in the presence of sizable and volatile capital inflows, without major financial crises and without imposing wider systemic risks. Large and volatile capital flows can exaggerate risk exposures and impair the ability of both banks and supervisors to assess and manage risk adequately.

Before discussing these important issues, this subsection examines the impact capital inflows have had on the domestic banking systems in selected APEC developing countries. The roles of central bank intervention and sterilization, which have a direct impact on bank balance sheets and the allocation of financial risk between the private and public sectors, are also examined.

Capital Inflows, Central Bank Intervention, and Domestic Credit Expansion

When capital flows into a developing economy as an increase in domestic bank foreign liabilities, the impact on the banking system is immediate: a local bank experiences an increase in foreign currency liabilities and obtains a foreign currency asset, usually in the form of a deposit in a bank chartered in a foreign currency market. If the local bank then extends a credit to an importer, the funds flow out of the market, causing no further expansion in domestic bank credit.[42] Alterna-

---

industrial countries known to have had recent banking problems. Among the Nordic countries, nonperforming loans as a percent of total commercial bank loans peaked in 1992 at 9 percent in Finland, 7 percent in Norway, and 8 percent in Sweden. In the United States, delinquent loans reached 6 percent of commercial bank loans in 1991. In Japan, the official estimate of nonperforming loans among the 21 major banks was 3 percent at end-March 1993.

[41]The savings and loan crisis in the United States and the banking crises in the Nordic countries are recent examples of how bad credit decisions can weaken the banking system. The recent debt and asset price deflations in many industrial countries illustrate how the combination of expansionary macroeconomic policies, rapid financial liberalization, and an inadequate supervisory and regulatory framework can lead to costly problems. See International Monetary Fund (1993) and Schinasi and Hargraves (1993).

[42]When the local bank lends funds to the importer, it simultaneously books a foreign currency loan and a foreign currency deposit to the importer. The local bank executes the transaction by drawing on its deposit in the foreign currency bank. At the end of the transaction, the local bank has a liability to the foreign currency bank and a foreign currency loan to the importer.

tively, the local central bank could purchase the foreign currency funds from the recipient bank, which would cause an increase in domestic currency bank reserves relative to the deposit base. If this transaction increases the reserve-deposit ratio above the legal minimum, banks can use their excess reserve position to increase bank credit.[43]

Even when capital flows into a developing country through nonbank financial asset markets, these transactions can affect the banking system as if there had been a direct expansion of bank liabilities.[44] When a nonresident invests in a nonbank financial asset, a local deposit must be used to pay for it, which involves exchanging a foreign currency deposit for a local currency deposit. In such transactions, the deposits and reserves of the domestic banking system are increased, at least temporarily. Hence, regardless of whether foreign capital flows into the market as foreign direct investment, equity portfolio investment, bond issuance, or bank borrowing, the increased deposits and bank reserves can lead to an increase in bank lending unless they are either used to import goods and/or assets or absorbed by the central bank through its sterilization policy. Moreover, the local bank and the local central bank have the same options as if the funds had entered the market through an increase in bank liabilities.

In principle, net capital inflows need not necessarily affect the domestic financial system permanently. At one extreme, the net inflow can finance an equivalent current account deficit, as when a nonresident purchases a domestic asset from a resident, who in turn uses the proceeds to import foreign goods. At the other extreme, the net capital inflow can be deposited within the banking system and completely sterilized by the central bank through a number of instruments. In each extreme case, net capital inflows do not affect the level of private domestic credit and only in the latter case will the composition of domestic financial assets and liabilities be altered.

In practice, net capital inflows have led to an expansion of domestic credit, reflecting the interplay of government policies, private investment decisions, and the behavior of financial institutions (including the financial infrastructure). In addition to determining the composition of assets and liabilities, the interaction of these decisions has also determined how assets and liabilities

are priced, who bears the financial risks, and how these risks are priced.

Central Bank Intervention and Sterilization

In 1993, one-third of the net capital inflows into the APEC developing countries were absorbed by the central bank in foreign currency reserves. Foreign currency reserves increase when the central bank directly purchases the foreign currency inflow, for example, as when it purchases foreign currencies from the banking system. The total accumulation of foreign currency reserves in any given period is a measure of the potential effect that net capital inflows can have on the total quantity of central bank reserves held by the banking system and, hence, on the level of domestic credit. In general, however, central banks have at their disposal several tools to sterilize the impact of capital inflows on the domestic economy and, in particular, on the pace of domestic credit expansion. Among them are direct instruments, such as increasing reserve requirements on commercial bank liabilities—to limit flows to the banking system or change the maturity structure of deposits—and indirect instruments, such as conducting open market operations and exchanging government bonds or central bank bills for foreign currency.[45]

Although reserve requirements have been used to sterilize inflows in some countries, they have two important disadvantages. First, to the extent that reserves are remunerated below market interest rates, they impose a tax on bank intermediation by increasing the wedge between interest rates on bank deposits and bank loans. Second, they may not be an effective tool for sterilizing capital inflows that are intermediated by nonbank financial institutions and by the capital markets, such as in the case of bond or equity portfolio flows.

Reserve requirements appear to have been an important direct instrument through which APEC developing countries have sterilized capital inflows.[46] For instance, Malaysia has relied on reserve requirements to absorb some of the excess liquidity generated by large capital inflows. The statutory reserve requirement was increased from 6.5 percent in 1991 to 8.5 percent in 1993 and has been raised more recently to 11.5 percent. Some of the resulting increase in the cost of funds

---

[43]If the local authorities permit residents to hold foreign currency deposits, the foreign currency deposit base can be expanded by the same process.

[44]For example, most of the bond portfolio inflows, which have dominated portfolio inflows into APEC developing countries in recent years, originated in the Euromarkets and are denominated in one of the major currencies. Thus, when nonresidents purchase Eurobonds issued by APEC borrowers, they transfer foreign currency deposits to APEC borrowers. If these borrowers hold their deposits in the local banking system, bond purchases have the same impact on the domestic financial system as a direct increase in domestic bank foreign liabilities.

[45]The need to limit the impact of capital inflows on the money supply is more pronounced for countries that operate fixed or managed exchange rate regimes, which is the case of many APEC developing countries.

[46]The effectiveness of reserve requirements depends on whether investors are able to circumvent them. In many industrial countries, investors can avoid reserve requirements by acquiring financial assets that are close substitutes for bank deposits, such as money market mutual funds, and thereby render sterilization ineffective. In most developing countries, however, close substitutes for bank deposits do not exist and so reserve requirements can often be used as an effective sterilization tool.

was passed through to borrowers and lenders, as the margin between deposit and lending rates increased from 3.8 percent to 4.7 percent.[47] Reserve requirements have also been used extensively in countries in the Western Hemisphere that have experienced large capital flows. For example, in 1992 Chile imposed a reserve requirement of 30 percent on all foreign credits, and Mexico restricted foreign currency liabilities of commercial banks to 10 percent of total liabilities.[48]

By increasing the cost of funds to some institutions, sterilization through reserve requirements can place banks at a competitive disadvantage vis-à-vis nonbank financial institutions, which often are not subject to the same regulations. Over time, bank disintermediation may occur as nonbanks replace banks as a source of private credit at more competitive rates. In Korea, for example, the central bank minimized the impact of increased liquidity on the financial system primarily by imposing high nonremunerated reserve requirements on commercial banks and by tightly regulating the market for bank credit.[49] This policy shifted deposits from banks to nonbanks, which were able to offer higher deposit rates; about 36 percent of deposit liabilities were held by deposit money banks in 1992, compared with over 70 percent in the 1970s. In the Philippines, very high reserve requirements, averaging 22 percent between 1987 and 1992, have been partly responsible for the low level of bank intermediation in the financial system.

Where sterilization has been conducted through indirect instruments, such as open market operations, its effectiveness has been limited by the ability of domestic securities and money markets to absorb the sale of government securities or central bank bills. In Korea, for example, the quantity of monetary stabilization bonds (MSBs) used by the central bank to sterilize inflows of foreign currencies increased from 9.6 percent of M2 in 1986 to 21 percent in 1992. In the last three years, Malaysia relied extensively on sales of central bank securities and on money market intervention to reduce liquidity. Such policies have often been associated with high and rising quasi-fiscal costs (the cases of Chile and Malaysia stand out in this regard) as domestic short-term interest rates have remained well above international levels.[50] Furthermore, it has been

argued that the relatively high short-term interest rates have acted as a stimulus to short-term inflows (Bercuson and Koenig (1993) and Calvo, Leiderman, and Reinhart (1993)).

Singapore and Malaysia (and other APEC developing countries) have used mechanisms other than reserve requirements or open market operations to sterilize capital inflows. One approach has involved moving the government's excess savings between bank accounts and government bonds to minimize the impact of capital flows on banks' balance sheets and prevent bank disintermediation. The Monetary Authority of Singapore did not hold government bonds for use in open market operations and was reluctant to burden banks with high reserve requirements. Instead, it sterilized capital flows and managed liquidity through portfolio allocations of the Central Provident Fund (CPF), a government-administered compulsory pension fund. The extensive savings in the CPF, which were invested primarily in government bonds, and large government budget surpluses allowed the central bank to control liquidity effectively.

A similar scheme was employed in Malaysia, where the central bank manages liquidity in part through the Employee Provident Fund (EPF), which holds about 20 percent of financial assets in the country. The authorities sterilized capital inflows by transferring government and EPF deposits from the banking system to special accounts in the central bank. As a result, federal and state government deposits held at the central bank increased from 3 percent of total deposits in 1989 to 19 percent in mid-1992. This sterilization effort expanded central bank liabilities relative to the monetary base and it might still have been inflationary. At the same time, however, Malaysia pursued a policy of fiscal consolidation, which was combined with early repayment of external debt.

During the financial reform in 1988–93, Indonesia sterilized capital inflows by actively managing the deposits of public enterprises, which were obliged to convert commercial bank deposits into Bank Indonesia certificates (SBIs). During this period, the outstanding stock of SBIs increased from 8 percent of the total liabilities of Bank Indonesia to 34 percent. Although these sterilization measures were successful in curbing excess liquidity, they also eroded the deposits of state-owned enterprises and sharply raised their funding cost.

In Taiwan Province of China, the authorities forced commercial banks to buy treasury bills and central bank certificates of deposit and shifted postal savings from the domestic banking system to the central bank. The central bank's balance sheet expanded and the ability of banks to intermediate financial flows weakened. Korea and Thailand attempted to sterilize capital inflows by encouraging outflows through the early repayment of external debt. Thailand also followed a

---

[47]Between 1991 and 1993, the cost of maintaining reserves at the central bank is estimated to have increased by about 23.5 percent, whereas the margin increased by 22.7 percent during this period.

[48]These restrictions were relaxed later in the year.

[49]In 1986, short-term money instruments (monetary stabilization bonds) were also introduced to manage liquidity. However, the central bank continues to impose high reserves ratios (11.5 percent) on demand and time deposits.

[50]In the case of Chile, the quasi-fiscal costs associated with intervention policies are estimated to have been 1.4 percent of GDP; see Kiguel and Leiderman (1994).

policy of fiscal restraint combined with increased government deposits at the central bank.[51]

Impact of Capital Inflows on Domestic Credit in Selected APEC Countries

As noted earlier, one-third of the capital that flowed into the APEC developing countries in 1993 was absorbed into foreign currency reserves; this reserve accumulation potentially represented an increase in domestic credit unless it was sterilized. The impact of net capital inflows on domestic credit expansions has differed markedly in individual APEC developing countries, however. In Korea, there were significant capital inflows in 1987 and 1991–92, but only in the earlier period did these result in a large overall payments balance; inflows in the latter period were largely offset by current account deficits. In Taiwan Province of China, large capital inflows in 1986-87 have been followed by large capital outflows. The Philippines did not experience significant capital inflows compared with its current account deficits until 1992. Consequently, capital inflows have not had great potential for altering the level of domestic credit in these countries. In Indonesia, Malaysia, Singapore, and Thailand, however, the difference between net capital inflows and the current account deficit—the overall balance, which primarily reflects reserve accumulation—was strongly positive, and it may be that the impact of capital inflows on the domestic banking system is greatest in these countries.

Countries that have experienced the greatest net capital inflows have also experienced rapid expansions in the commercial bank sectors (Table 4-1). In Thailand, for example, bank assets expanded rapidly in relation to GDP after 1987, from 73 percent of GDP in 1988 to 102 percent in 1993. Similar experiences occurred in Indonesia, where assets expanded from 45 percent of GDP in 1988 to 74 percent in 1993, and in Malaysia, where this ratio increased from 118 percent in 1992 to 134 percent in 1993.

In addition to intermediating capital inflows, commercial banks themselves imported substantial amounts of foreign capital. As a result, commercial bank gross foreign liabilities generally rose as a percent of GDP: in Indonesia, from 2 percent in 1989 to 7 percent in 1993; in Malaysia, from 7 percent in 1990 to 19 percent in 1993; and in Thailand, from 3 percent in 1987 to 11 percent in 1993. In each country, the source of the greatest growth in liabilities was borrowing from foreign financial institutions, and not the accumulation of foreign currency deposits, although reserve accumulation was significant in Indonesia.

The banking sectors in these countries also expanded through a direct increase in domestic deposits. Since 1988, nongovernment domestic deposits grew significantly in relation to GDP in both Indonesia and Thailand and at a slightly slower pace in Malaysia (see Table 4-1). Deposit growth generally increased after the onset of capital inflows, and, in Indonesia and Thailand, provided the impetus for about two-thirds of the expansion of the banking sector. By contrast, in Malaysia, growth in deposits remained subdued until around 1992–93, when deposits rose sharply from 63 percent of GDP in 1992 to 72 percent in 1993.

In all three countries, the increase in deposits and foreign liabilities more than compensated for reductions in central bank credit and government deposits; moreover, these reductions were often implemented deliberately as part of sterilization programs. In Malaysia, government deposits in commercial banks declined by 72 percent between 1989 and 1993, while in Thailand and Indonesia, government deposits grew but not as quickly as total liabilities. Similarly, central bank credit to commercial banks declined in nominal terms in both Indonesia and Thailand. A more detailed examination of bank assets suggests that funds were directed mostly toward domestic investments. Gross foreign assets declined in relation to GDP in Indonesia and Malaysia and increased slightly in Thailand (see Table 4-1). In all three countries, foreign assets declined as a share of total assets, with the result that net foreign assets declined sharply and in all three cases led to a net liability position. For example, commercial bank net foreign assets declined in Malaysia from less than 1.5 percent of GDP in 1989 to a net liability of 13 percent in 1993 (Table 4-1). In Indonesia, a net foreign asset position of 4.5 percent of GDP in 1989 turned to a net liability position of 3 percent in 1993; similarly, in Thailand, a near-balanced position at the end of 1987 swung to a net foreign liability position of 6 percent of GDP in 1993.

The net result in some cases was a strong expansion in domestic lending. Loans to the domestic private sector in Thailand increased from 51 percent of GDP in 1988 to 79 percent in 1993; in Indonesia they increased from 27 percent of GDP to 55 percent. In Malaysia, lending to the private sector expanded modestly, actually declining as a proportion of total assets. Banks in Malaysia have invested funds in the interbank market by holding excess reserves at the central bank, which pays the interbank interest rate on such deposits. Loans to other banks in Malaysia rose from 8 percent of total assets in 1991 to 22 percent in 1993.

In Malaysia and Thailand, the expansion in domestic lending coincided with a reduction in holdings of government securities and an increase in holdings of private sector securities. Although banks' holdings of all securities as a share of assets or GDP did not rise significantly in Malaysia, and actually fell sharply in

---

[51]The government deposits held at the Bank of Thailand increased from 25 percent of total deposits in 1987 to 82 percent in mid-1992.

Table 4-1. Indicators of Banking Activity in Selected APEC Countries
(In percent of GDP)

	1985	1986	1987	1988	1989	1990	1991	1992	1993
Indonesia									
Assets of deposit money banks	34.7	39.7	38.6	44.5	55.6	67.8	67.4	70.2	74.3
Loans to private sector	17.4	21.2	22.5	27.4	36.4	49.8	51.7	50.9	54.9
Nongovernment deposits	19.1	21.5	22.1	25.0	30.6	38.5	39.3	41.1	43.9
Foreign assets	6.4	8.0	6.3	5.9	6.4	6.0	4.9	5.0	3.8
Foreign liabilities	0.6	0.5	0.6	0.8	1.9	6.5	5.2	6.2	6.6
Korea									
Assets of commercial banks	70.4	63.9	62.2	59.1	61.2	75.5	74.9	75.1	73.4
Loans to private sector	47.3	46.6	47.4	48.3	51.6	58.3	57.0	55.8	54.6
Nongovernment deposits	23.1	23.0	26.2	28.6	28.1	33.3	31.7	30.2	30.0
Holdings of government securities	1.1	1.2	1.2	1.3	1.2	1.6	1.6	1.0	1.0
Holdings of nongovernment securities	2.0	2.4	2.4	2.1	3.3	4.8	4.8	5.5	6.5
Foreign assets	4.7	3.8	3.5	3.2	2.7	3.7	3.6	4.0	4.6
Foreign liabilities	10.2	7.9	5.7	3.9	3.5	4.0	4.8	4.7	4.4
Malaysia									
Assets of commercial banks	95.7	110.8	106.4	106.5	109.8	111.6	117.3	117.6	134.0
Loans to private sector	62.5	72.4	64.6	61.4	64.4	68.8	74.2	70.9	69.8
Nongovernment deposits	59.1	67.7	62.4	58.0	58.4	53.8	58.9	62.7	71.8
Holdings of government securities	8.6	9.0	11.8	13.0	10.7	9.3	8.7	7.0	5.7
Holdings of nongovernment securities	2.1	3.2	4.6	5.5	4.3	6.2	8.3	8.9	11.0
Foreign assets	3.9	5.4	6.3	8.1	7.7	6.6	5.0	3.6	6.3
Foreign liabilities	8.2	8.6	6.3	5.6	6.2	7.0	9.1	12.6	19.0
Philippines									
Assets of commercial banks	51.8	43.5	42.1	42.8	45.4	50.1	48.0	51.1	58.9
Loans to private sector	19.3	13.9	15.3	15.6	16.7	18.6	17.4	20.0	25.7
Nongovernment deposits	22.1	20.3	20.5	22.2	24.4	26.9	26.9	28.5	32.1
Holdings of government securities	2.5	3.6	3.4	4.5	5.6	5.1	4.5	6.1	5.3
Holdings of nongovernment securities	3.0	2.1	1.3	1.1	1.1	1.6	3.5	2.4	2.9
Foreign assets of commercial banks	7.3	7.4	8.1	8.8	8.6	10.3	8.5	8.8	9.1
Foreign liabilities of commercial banks	13.9	9.6	9.4	9.4	9.6	12.1	10.6	13.1	15.1
Taiwan Province of China									
Assets of deposit money banks	110.0	115.2	127.9	140.5	156.3	157.6	168.9	182.8	193.2
Loans to private sector	2.2	1.7	1.6	1.7	1.5	1.4	1.3	1.3	1.2
Nongovernment deposits	2.8	2.4	2.1	2.0	1.8	1.7	1.5	1.3	1.3
Holdings of government securities	1.5	1.5	1.9	2.9	2.3	1.9	3.1	4.6	5.5
Holdings of nongovernment securities	13.0	22.2	33.3	21.9	19.0	14.8	17.8	13.6	16.0
Foreign assets	14.8	8.6	4.6	5.5	6.6	8.4	7.8	6.3	6.4
Foreign liabilities	5.4	9.9	13.3	10.4	8.2	7.1	8.2	7.4	7.8
Thailand									
Assets of commercial banks	67.5	68.5	72.6	73.4	76.8	82.5	86.6	91.0	102.4
Loans to private sector	45.5	44.2	47.3	51.0	56.3	64.3	67.7	72.8	79.1
Nongovernment deposits	50.0	52.9	55.4	54.9	58.5	63.4	67.1	68.9	73.2
Holdings of government securities	7.3	9.2	8.8	7.9	6.5	5.0	3.2	2.4	1.5
Holdings of nongovernment securities	0.8	1.0	1.0	1.1	1.2	1.2	2.5	2.9	3.6
Foreign assets	3.2	3.7	3.0	2.9	3.8	2.6	2.9	2.8	5.0
Foreign liabilities	4.3	2.8	2.9	4.0	4.6	5.0	4.9	6.0	11.2

Sources: Bangko Sentral ng Pilipinas; Bank Indonesia; Bank of Korea; Bank Negara Malaysia; Bank of Thailand; Central Bank of China (Taiwan Province of China); and IMF staff estimates.

Thailand, in both countries bank investment in private securities more than doubled as a proportion of assets and/or GDP between 1989 and 1993.

This brief discussion of bank balance sheets suggests the following general observations: (1) the period of high net capital inflows coincided with an increase in liabilities of the banking sector, often driven by foreign borrowing; (2) these sources of funds allowed banks to expand their balance sheets despite a reduction in funding from the central bank and the government; and (3) these funds were allocated mostly to domestic lending, with some increase in private sector securities investment.

Risk Allocation Between the Public and Private Sectors

The decision to sterilize capital inflows implies that the balance sheet of the central bank, rather than that of the banking system, will expand. This effectively transfers risk from the banking system to the central bank. Because of the high cost of sterilization, and the high potential public cost of financial losses, careful consideration must be given to the allocation of risk between the private and public sectors.

When the banking system is sound and efficient and there is effective regulatory and supervisory control over banks, then capital flows will not create additional risks to the financial system or increase the probability of financial problems. When extending credit, banks are able to anticipate the effect of a reversal of capital flows on the revenues of their borrowers (interest rate and exchange rate risks) by pricing loans accordingly, accumulating reserves against such loans, and reducing the concentration of their loan portfolios to sectors that may be affected by such reversals.

In contrast, when credit institutions operate in a regulatory environment that allows them to misallocate credit and mismanage their balance sheets, an expansion of bank credit induced by capital inflows will create further opportunities for banks to expose the financial system to a larger risk of financial loss. In pursuing a policy of nonsterilization in such weak systems, the central bank runs the risk that it may have to provide liquidity or equity to troubled or insolvent banks. Moreover, in the event of a reversal of capital flows, weak banks would become especially vulnerable. Owing to their poor credit ratings, the weaker financial institutions would be unable to access the market and would need central bank support. The history of bank crises, including the recent crisis in the industrial countries, clearly demonstrates how high the public costs of such rescue operations can be.[52]

---

[52]In the Nordic countries, public funds (including deposit insurance funds) were expended during 1991–93 to resolve the banking crises. As a share of 1992 GDP, these public expenditures amounted to 8 percent in Finland, 4 percent in Norway, and 6 percent in Sweden. In 1992, the estimated total cost of resolving the U.S. savings and loan crisis and problems in the commercial banking industry was nearly 4 percent of GDP. The large capital flows in Chile in the late 1970s, combined with the full state guarantee to bank deposits and the ownership of banks by industrial or financial conglomerates to which cheap credit was granted, led to the banking crisis in 1982, after the economy was subject to external shocks. The cost of rescuing the banks over the period 1982–85 has been estimated at 44 percent of Chile's 1985 GDP. See Fischer and Reisen (1992).

Banking Sector, Infrastructure, and Capital Inflows

The relatively recent experiences of some of the APEC developing countries suggest that the combination of immature infrastructures, relatively weak regulatory structures, and external influences—for example, terms of trade shocks and economic recession—can strain domestic financial systems, lead to financial crisis, and impose severe real economic costs. The recent surges in capital inflows and the potential for further increases, or for a rapid reversal of these flows, can pose similar risks.

Although a thorough discussion of experiences with banking crises in individual countries is beyond the scope of this section, many of the problems that have led to financial crises are common to other APEC countries that are now experiencing sizable and volatile capital inflows. After briefly reviewing recent financial crises in selected APEC countries, and drawing relevant lessons from them, this subsection briefly discusses common areas where supervisory and regulatory frameworks can be improved and also discusses recent regulatory reforms in some of the countries. The challenges these countries will face in improving the banking sectors in the period ahead are then summarized.

Financial Crises and Inadequate Infrastructure

In many of the APEC developing countries, interest rate liberalization and bank deregulation led to greater access to funds, and greater competition among banks for these funds—as capital inflows have done more recently—well before the regulatory and supervisory frameworks were improved and before they were capable of adequately safeguarding against systemic risk. In Indonesia and Malaysia, for example, banking crises emerged after significant deregulation measures were implemented in the late 1970s and early 1980s. Although the impetus for many of these measures was terms of trade shocks, these shocks and recessions in the early to mid-1980s exposed the weaknesses in bank balance sheets, including the illiquidity of a large proportion of loans made during the period of increased competition. Improvements in prudential regulation were implemented after a crisis had developed, and in some other countries, regulations specifying the definition of bank capital, provisioning requirements for various classes of substandard assets, and the levels of lending and exposure limits were promulgated only in the late 1980s. The absence of adequate regulation and supervision meant that inherited poor practices were not corrected and that banks were not adequately provisioned against potential loan losses when recession hit. At the same time, the greater competition introduced by the initial reforms made it less possible for banks to earn their way out of financial trouble by widening interest margins.

The structural weaknesses in many banking systems that surface in times of financial stress—and that might surface during periods of large and volatile capital flows—can be traced, in part, to the use of commercial bank loans to achieve government economic policy objectives. Many of the APEC developing countries, including Indonesia, Korea, Malaysia, the Philippines, and Thailand, some of which have experienced surges of inflows, have regulatory requirements to allocate fixed proportions of bank loan portfolios to particular sectors.[53] Such practices can be inconsistent with sound banking practices: mandated loans are often refinanced by the central bank at relatively favorable rates, and banks therefore have little incentive to assess and price their credit risk properly. Furthermore, when banks have difficulty meeting their lending requirements, these loans are inevitably extended to projects with high risk and regardless of cash flow. In some countries, the Philippines for example, banks can substitute purchases of government bonds for lending to priority sectors; however, these bonds generally pay below-market interest rates. In addition, because banks are often not required to identify properly, and to provide reserves against, problem loans, banks in many of these countries carried bad loans as performing and capitalized unpaid interest. When economic growth slowed in the mid-1980s and financial stresses emerged, a large proportion of these loans became nonperforming, which weakened bank balance sheets and created the potential for sizable quasi-fiscal costs.

Another problem that has arisen in some APEC developing countries is that aggregate bank lending has at times become highly concentrated in particular economic sectors. This concentration of lending increased the vulnerability of the banking system, and of the financial system, to sector-specific economic developments. Even though aggregate balance sheet data are not generally detailed enough to evaluate country risk accurately, they can indicate where there is a high concentration of lending to particular sectors.[54] In Thailand, for example, the share of bank credit extended to the construction and real estate sectors—two sectors that are typically known to be risky and vulnerable to interest rate changes—has increased sharply since the surge in capital inflows, rising steadily from 8 percent in 1980 to 16 percent in 1990, where it has remained. Most of the increase in lending was for real estate transactions, and so the surge in net capital inflows in 1988–90 appears to have been associated with a significant increase in exposure to property values. As the experience in many industrial countries in recent years has shown—including the United States and Japan—even when the initial collateral value of the land exceeds the value of the loan by a wide margin, significant exposures to commercial property can seriously impair the strength of the bank balance sheets if property prices fall.

In Indonesia, balance sheet weakness in the private banking system was related to credit exposures to borrowers connected to the lending bank. Although there were regulatory restrictions on bank ownership, they did not prevent banks from becoming controlled by nonfinancial firms.[55] In addition, extensive lending to bank-related borrowers, with little attention to their capacity to repay, was responsible, in large part, for the accumulation of nonperforming loans on the balance sheets of the private banks. In Malaysia, there were no regulations in the 1980s that governed credit exposures either to single counterparties or to borrowers connected to the bank. Unsecured loans to individuals became nonperforming during the recession in 1985 and the associated severe liquidity shortage. Other sources of bad loans were bank-credit exposures to the property sector and bank credits backed by equity shares, which became nonperforming as a result of the asset price deflation in Malaysia in 1985.

Finally, in general, increased access to an international market might have made it easier for the most creditworthy firms to tap international markets directly by issuing stocks or bonds; this form of financing has soared in recent years. As a result, banks in many of the APEC developing countries may be lending to second-tier, high-risk customers.

The lessons from these experiences for the APEC developing countries are clear: (1) in periods of macroeconomic instability, rapid financial change, and market volatility—such as with surges in capital inflows and the strains they can place on the domestic financial systems—long-standing inefficiencies come to light, such as information and incentive problems, poor cred-

---

[53]In Korea, the main objective during the 1970s was to ensure funding for heavy industry. Since then, the emphasis has switched toward small and medium-sized enterprises. In Malaysia, the main objective has been to ensure access to credit by the Bumiputera population and by small-scale enterprises. In Indonesia, the Philippines, and Thailand, small-scale and agricultural borrowers were the target. These loans were often funded by the authorities directly (as in Korea through government funds allocated to the banks) or indirectly through central bank rediscounting, and usually carried interest rates well below those paid by other borrowers. In Korea, policy loans accounted for almost half of nationwide commercial bank loans through the 1970s and 1980s and even in 1990, almost ten years after these banks were privatized (see Nam (1993)). In some of the other countries, the aggregated policy lending requirements reached similar proportions of total commercial bank lending.

[54]A true picture of risk exposures can be obtained only from detailed audits of bank balance sheets.

[55]See Nasution (1993). Other examples are Korea and Taiwan Province of China, where the use of dummy accounts and borrowed names is widespread. In these circumstances, it is not possible to enforce restrictions against concentrations of lending to the bank shareholders.

it assessment, inadequate risk management, and other weaknesses in the infrastructure, in particular in the supervisory and regulatory frameworks; and (2) to avoid such problems in the future—caused either by even greater capital inflows or by reversals of such flows—careful and timely examinations of existing supervisory and regulatory frameworks are needed, and structural changes may be required to strengthen prudential supervision.

Weaknesses in the Supervisory and Regulatory Infrastructure

The recent financial history of many of the APEC developing countries, as well as other evidence, suggests that many of these countries are not well equipped to manage the increased risks inherent in intermediating volatile capital flows and to absorb high asset price volatility. Many financial institutions remain subject to moral hazard: aspects of the regulatory regime, such as deposit insurance in the Philippines and Taiwan Province of China or central bank rediscounting of credits to priority sectors, can weaken incentives to manage risks because the costs of loan losses are not borne entirely by the bank. Related incentive problems exist in countries such as Indonesia, the Philippines, and Taiwan Province of China, where state-owned banks play a significant role in the intermediation process. State-owned institutions may have less of an incentive to manage risk properly because the presumption of a public sector bailout may be greater for a failed state-owned institution than for a failed private bank. Even in private institutions, internal risk management may be inadequate. The essence of internal control is the measurement and assessment of risk exposures (including the creditworthiness of the borrowers and market risk) and the implementation of banking practices that make these risks manageable. Poor accounting standards and limited information disclosure requirements make the assessment of the riskiness of creditors very difficult. Accounting standards are widely perceived as being relatively weak in many APEC developing countries. In Indonesia, there are as yet no standards to ensure consistent financial reporting across banks, and similar problems exist in Taiwan Province of China. Similarly, in the Philippines, auditors have limited power to examine company records: they are dependent upon their clients to provide the necessary information and face no penalty if the information reported is incorrect. In many countries, reliable information is available only for the very largest listed companies, particularly those that have accessed foreign capital markets. Even in these cases, the use of borrowed names, as in Korea or Taiwan Province of China, or the maintenance of multiple accounts greatly diminishes the reliability of reported information (see

Sudibyo and others (1994), Shea (1993), and Lamberte and Llanto (1993)).

The lack of enforcement of existing regulations is a source of problems in many developing countries. A minimum requirement of an effectively operating bank is that there is independent internal oversight of lending decisions by a credit review committee. Such oversight would provide a check against abuses such as lending in excess of loan approval or credit exposure limits. An equally important contribution of the review process is the subsequent follow-up as part of a systematic effort to monitor the quality of the loan portfolio. This management role is often lacking in developing country banking systems, which makes it difficult to obtain a comprehensive picture of the extent to which loans are nonperforming or at risk of becoming nonperforming.

The supervisory and regulatory infrastructures in APEC developing countries are often ill equipped to assess and manage the systemic risks inherent in immature financial systems, especially in the presence of large and volatile capital flows.[56] The general requirements of a sound prudential regulatory structure include vesting the supervisory agency with the authority to examine bank operations and balance sheets, inject liquidity or capital into banks to contain financial crises, close banks and restrict dividend payments, issue cease and desist orders, establish entry criteria and capital adequacy rules, define exposure limits, delineate and enforce permitted and prohibited activities, and enforce asset classification and provisioning rules. An important contribution of bank supervision is to relate the true economic value of a bank's portfolio to its capital base, and bank supervision and examination must, therefore, focus on identifying and resolving problem assets. Poor accounting standards may mean, however, that banks have inadequate information about the quality of their loan portfolios and that even detailed examinations by supervisors and regulators may not reveal more information.

Current regulations governing the reporting of asset quality fall short of international practices in a number of APEC developing countries. Malaysia, for example, has only an elementary loan classification system, and loans must be six months in arrears before they are classified as nonperforming—the same allowance as given in Taiwan Province of China. In Thailand, there appear to be no requirements to classify loans, and, in all three countries required loan-loss provisions are relatively low. In the Philippines, the loan classification system appears to leave considerable discretion to bank

---

[56]The Appendix contains summary descriptions of essential elements of commercial bank regulations drawn, in most cases, from published sources only. Errors and omissions may exist where relevant information is not readily available or, as in the case of Taiwan Province of China, where there is no official contact with the International Monetary Fund.

management to decide how to classify loans.[57] In addition, regulators in some countries may have no credible legal recourse against banks that fail to comply with regulations. Central banks, for example, may not have the authority to close insolvent banks, seize assets, or issue cease and desist orders.

Most of the APEC developing countries have introduced modified risk-based capital requirements in recent years. If banks are not required to report accurately on the condition of their asset portfolios, however, then capital requirements are ineffective. To avoid capital losses on nonperforming loans, banks will record interest as accrued. Additional problems may arise owing to liberal or unclear definitions of what can be included in capital. As a result, high capital-adequacy ratios in countries with weak disclosure requirements often disguise bad loans.

To avoid loan losses, bank regulators in most APEC developing countries have imposed limits on bank lending in a variety of forms, including liquidity requirements and exposure limits.[58] In Indonesia, banks may not provide credits in excess of 20 percent of bank capital to any one borrower or 50 percent to any group of borrowers. In Thailand, the limit on lending to any one debtor is 25 percent of capital and that on receiving commitments from the same borrower is 50 percent. In the Philippines, the limit on single borrowers is 25 percent of capital unless the loan is secured by risk-free assets. In Taiwan Province of China, banks may not lend in excess of their deposits. There are, however, no other limits on lending to individual borrowers other than those on loans to bank insiders. In most of the countries, there are statutory limits or prohibitions on lending to directors or other officers of the bank and, in some cases, these apply to their families and the companies they own.

Such controls are easily circumvented in countries where regulations and accounting practices are weak. For example, in Korea, until September 1993, it was legal to use a fictitious name when transacting with a financial institution. As a result, there was no way to enforce restrictions on loans to individual counterparties or bank insiders. As was noted above, the use of dummy accounts or borrowed names is not uncommon in other countries, including the Philippines and Taiwan

Province of China. Moreover, in Malaysia until 1986 and in the Philippines until relatively recently, for example, bank examiners lacked the authority to trace the use of funds once they were deposited in accounts, so it was not possible to prevent borrowers from passing the proceeds on to others who were not eligible for loans.

Strong legal and accounting systems are important elements of the regulatory support for risk management. In many developing countries, debtors enjoy strong protection from the courts, which reduces the effectiveness of bank claims to seize collateral in the event that the loans are not properly serviced. Bankruptcy proceedings are frequently an inefficient way of resolving bank claims. In the Philippines, for example, the Insolvency Law lists bank claims last among 14 categories of preferences for the settlement of claims on the assets of a bankrupt firm. There is often no separate judicial structure that specializes in commercial law, with the result that courts may not be well equipped to adjudicate such disputes. In addition, it is common for there to be no registration of collateral claims: lenders must take physical possession of collateral—which eliminates the use of land as collateral—to enforce their claims and to be sure that there are no other claims on the same assets.

Deregulation and Capital Inflows

While capital inflows were frequently encouraged by deregulation measures, the negative impact they appear to have had on financial institutions in some countries has led to two types of response. One response, adopted by Malaysia for example, has been to try to reverse temporarily the factors that attracted foreign capital in the first place. In the past year, Bank Negara Malaysia has imposed limits on the size of banks' foreign currency swap books and on their overall foreign liabilities. For a few months in 1994, residents were not permitted to sell short-term securities to nonresidents. In addition, foreign financial institutions' accounts in Malaysian banks had to be deposited in accounts with the central bank that did not pay interest and were subject to reserve requirements; this resulted in a high tax on nonresident deposits. The reserve requirement on these accounts was lifted in May, and the ban on issues of short-term securities to nonresidents was rescinded in August.

By contrast, in Indonesia, pressures from foreign capital flows have been used to promote deregulation and reforms in the domestic markets. The initial round of interest rate deregulation in 1983 was prompted by external pressures, which in Malaysia had contributed to the imposition of new controls on bank lending rates in that year (see Cole (1993)). More recently, the Indonesian authorities have not attempted to constrain inflows—reserve requirements have not been raised as they have in Malaysia, for example—but they have

---

[57]In the United States, nonperforming loans include all loans that are at least 90 days overdue and all "substandard" and "loss" loans. In Japan, nonperforming loans are defined as loans to bankrupt borrowers and loans that are 180 days or more overdue.

[58]In the European Union, banks face a limit of 25 percent of capital on each of their large exposures—a transitional limit of 40 percent is applied in some cases—with the added condition that all exposures in excess of 10 percent of capital may not exceed eight times capital. In the United States, the large exposure limit is 15 percent of capital plus surplus, and in Japan the limit on exposures of ordinary banks to single borrowers and their subsidiaries is 40 percent of equity.

tried to ensure their proper intermediation by improving prudential regulations and by sterilizing when necessary. One cost of this openness has been that the initial reduction in interest rates when capital inflows surged and their subsequent increase when sterilization was strengthened appear to have added to the asset quality problems in the banking system. Nonperforming loans in the large state-owned banks reportedly increased from 6 percent of loans at the end of 1990 to 21 percent as of October 1993.

The timing of reform measures suggests that an important objective of financial liberalization was the improved access to, and use of, foreign capital (Cole (1993)). The simultaneity, in some countries, of financial deregulation and liberalization of external capital flows supports this conjecture. More directly, in Indonesia, between 1979 and 1991, the central bank, Bank Indonesia, encouraged foreign exchange inflows through the banking system by conducting foreign currency swaps with the banks—on demand—at a forward premium that was set below the expected rate of depreciation. Before 1989, banks were subject to a system of complex ceilings on foreign borrowing. Between March 1989 and 1991, this policy was combined with limits on daily net open foreign exchange positions amounting to 25 percent of capital (reduced to 20 percent in 1991). The change in policy, combined with the subsidy on the forward premium, induced inflows of short-term capital, which Bank Indonesia could not sterilize because of the shallowness of the money market (see Nasution (1993)). In 1990, monetary policy was tightened (interest rates on SBI bills rose from 17.7 percent in March 1990 to 21.5 percent in March 1991), and the forward premium subsidy was cut substantially. The ceilings on foreign borrowing were reintroduced in October 1991, but private borrowers face only a reporting requirement, not an approval requirement.

In other countries, the ability of banks to accumulate foreign liabilities or domestic liabilities denominated in foreign currency was improved as part of the early deregulation process. Capital inflows were further encouraged by the relatively high interest rates that prevailed in the region. Although specific causes differed among countries, high interest rates were a direct result of such factors as monetary tightening, interest rate deregulation, the encouragement of competition among financial institutions, and the relatively high costs of intermediation.

Impact of Portfolio Capital Flows on Emerging Equity Markets

Capital began to flow in substantial amounts to the APEC developing countries in the late 1980s, mostly in the form of foreign direct investment (FDI). During the early 1990s, the composition of flows began to change markedly, and portfolio flows began to play an increasingly important role (Table 4-2). Net portfolio flows increased sharply in dollar terms in the 1990s and also rose as a share of total net capital inflows, from about 2 percent of net inflows in 1990 to about 42 percent in 1993. At the same time, "other" net capital inflows—which includes commercial bank lending—fell slightly in dollar terms and declined sharply as a share of total net inflows. Equity flows, which were negligible before 1989, rose significantly in the early 1990s, and bond flows surged, although most bond issues were raised in the Euromarkets and were not intermediated by the domestic bond markets in individual countries.

Table 4-2. Net Capital Flows to APEC Developing Countries[1]

	1990	1991	1992	1993
	(In billions of U.S. dollars)			
Net capital flows	26.6	51.9	43.3	89.4
Foreign direct investment	12.1	19.1	23.4	39.5
Portfolio investment	0.5	11.5	19.9	37.1
Other	14.1	21.3	—	12.8
	(In percent of net capital flows)			
Net capital flows	100.0	100.0	100.0	100.0
Foreign direct investment	45.5	36.8	54.0	44.2
Portfolio investment	1.9	22.2	46.0	41.5
Other	53.0	41.0	—	14.3

Sources: International Monetary Fund, *Balance of Payments Statistics Yearbook*; and IMF staff estimates.
[1]Net medium- and long-term capital, excluding exceptional financing and flows related to debt and debt-service reduction.

Table 4-3. Daily Market Index Return Volatility and Extreme Price Movement Analysis

	Absolute Volatility[1]	Relative Volatility[2]	Probability of Extreme Price Decline[3] (In percent)
Hong Kong			
Low-inflow period (Jan. 1988–Aug. 1991)	1.61	1.52	2.06
High-inflow period (Sept. 1991–Oct. 1993)	1.31	1.98	1.74
Volatile-flow period (Nov. 1993–July 1994)	2.33	3.68	9.94
Korea			
Low-inflow period (Jan. 1988–Dec. 1991)	1.51	1.42	3.22
High-inflow period (Jan. 1992–June 1993)	1.18	2.55	3.40
Volatile-flow period (July 1993–July 1994)	1.14	2.31	2.01
Thailand			
Volatile-flow period (Jan. 1988–Apr. 1991)	1.19	1.74	5.51
Moderate-inflow period (May 1991–Oct. 1992)	1.69	2.14	3.97
High-flow-volatility period (Nov. 1992–July 1994)	1.17	2.66	3.75
Mexico			
Low-inflow period (Jan. 1988–Apr. 1990)	1.99	1.88	5.11
Volatile-flow period (May 1990–Jan. 1993)	1.57	1.76	4.59
More-steady-inflow period (Feb. 1993–January 1994)	1.61	2.57	3.72

Source: IMF staff calculations from the WEFA Group Data Base.

Note: The separation of the overall sample into different subsample periods with different portfolio flow characteristics is performed by inspecting the monthly portfolio flow data from the United States to these emerging markets and the data on the changes in monthly flows. The separation is also jointly determined by the use of common structural-break test statistics including the CUSUM test statistics and the CUSUMSQ test statistics. The returns data are the continuously compounded daily returns from the Hang Seng Index for Hong Kong, the Korea Composite Index for Korea, the Bangkok SET Index for Thailand, and the Morgan Stanley Capital International Index for Mexico.

[1]Standard deviation of the daily return.
[2]Standard deviation relative to standard deviation of the daily return of the Dow Jones Industrial Average.
[3]Probability of a larger than 3 percent daily drop.

The benefits to APEC developing countries of greater access to global capital markets include lower funding costs—the result of diversification of funding sources—improved liquidity and market depth, and increased market efficiency.[59] However, these benefits of capital inflows can be offset, at least in part, by the possibility that the international integration of capital markets has exposed the smaller and less liquid stock markets to spillovers of turbulence from industrial country securities markets. In addition, the high volatility of equity prices in recipient countries has led to concerns about the impact of capital inflows on equity price volatility in these countries.[60] Moreover, many of the emerging markets have not yet had time to develop an adequate financial infrastructure, including

adequate accounting standards, disclosure requirements, trading mechanisms and exchanges, and clearing and settlement systems. The interaction of surges in capital flows and weaknesses in the financial infrastructure may increase systemic risks and, in some cases, lead to systemic problems in domestic markets. Finally, there is a question about whether market integrity and transparency in the capital markets of APEC developing countries are evolving quickly enough to retain the confidence of foreign investors in times of stress. These issues are discussed and some empirical analyses of spillover effects from foreign markets, of price volatility, and of market efficiency are provided.

Spillovers, Price Volatility, Market Liquidity, and Market Efficiency

Market Linkage and Spillovers

The increased participation of foreign investors can potentially strengthen the link between local and foreign markets. Although foreign participation might not

---

[59]See Feldman and Kumar (1994) for a discussion of the potential contributions equity markets can make to growth in developing countries.

[60]In addition, as Table 4-3 highlights, volatility in emerging markets, as measured by the standard deviation of stock returns, remains very high by industrial country standards. For the period January 1992 to July 1994, daily stock returns in these emerging markets were twice as variable as stock returns in the United States.

affect the relationships between market fundamentals in industrial and emerging stock markets, it can magnify the effect of industrial country market turbulence (as experienced in the first quarter of 1994) on the emerging equity markets (see International Monetary Fund (1994)).

Spillovers increase when the behavior of nonresident investors leads to a defensive investment strategy by resident investors. Because local investors generally have no information about whether foreign investors are changing their portfolios because of liquidity constraints, rediversification, or special information about economic fundamentals, local investors will tend to react to such moves. Such reactions will magnify the effect of foreign turbulence on the local market.

To examine whether volatility spillovers have increased recently, Table 4-4 reports correlations between stock price volatility in the United States on one day and stock price volatility in emerging stock markets on the following day. Volatility is estimated by the squared daily stock market return. As Table 4-4 shows, volatility has spilled over from the U.S. stock market to the emerging stock markets, and these spillovers have been strongest when portfolio flows have been most volatile.[61] The correlation measures of volatility spillovers are highest during the volatile-flow periods in all countries examined except Thailand. For both Hong Kong and Korea, the correlation measure of volatility spillovers in the volatile-flow period is more than twice as large as in the low-inflow period. For Mexico, the correlation measure of volatility spillovers in the volatile-flow period (which occurs in a different time period than those of Hong Kong and Korea) is about seven times the correlation measure for the low-inflow period.

Increase in Market Volatility

The presence of foreign investors can also increase stock price volatility by magnifying price fluctuations in the local market. Outflows are likely to occur when small and illiquid markets are weak. Investors tend to redeem their shares from the fund, and fund managers are then obliged to sell shares in the local market, which further depresses prices. In this way, the participation of large mutual funds—which in some countries is the only way for nonresidents to invest—might have a destabilizing impact on the local market. In December 1993, for example, U.S. investors purchased $674 million worth of Hong Kong shares on a net basis; however, in the following month, U.S. investors sold,

---

[61]The increase in volatility spillover in Mexico, when portfolio flows became volatile, is statistically significant at the 1 percent level (see Table 4-4). The subsequent drop in spillover, when portfolio flows became less volatile, is also highly significant. In Thailand, there was a significant drop in volatility spillovers when portfolio flows became less volatile.

Table 4-4. Volatility Spillover Analysis

	Correlation Measure of Volatility Spillover[1]
Hong Kong	
Low-inflow period (Jan. 1988–Aug. 1991)	0.068 **
High-inflow period (Sept. 1991–Oct. 1993)	0.023
Volatile-flow period (Nov. 1993–July 1994)	0.150 * +
Korea	
Low-inflow period (Jan. 1988–Dec. 1991)	0.055 *
High-inflow period (Jan. 1992–June 1993)	0.029
Volatile-flow period (July 1993–July 1994)	0.120 *
Thailand	
Volatile-flow period (Jan. 1988–Apr. 1991)	0.296 ***
Moderate-inflow period (May 1991–Oct. 1992)	0.115 ** +++
High-flow-volatility period (Nov. 1992–July 1994)	0.103 **
Mexico	
Low-inflow period (Jan. 1988–Apr. 1990)	0.048
Volatile-flow period (May 1990–Jan. 1993)	0.324 *** +++
More-steady-inflow period (Feb. 1993–July 1994)	0.003 +++

Source: IMF staff calculations from the WEFA Group Data Base.

Note: The separation of the overall sample into different subsample periods with different portfolio flow characteristics is performed by inspecting the monthly portfolio flow data from the United States to these emerging markets and the data on the changes in monthly flows. The separation is also jointly determined by the use of common structural-break test statistics, including the CUSUM test statistics and the CUSUMSQ test statistics. The return data are the continuously compounded daily return from the Hang Seng Index for Hong Kong, the Korea Composite Index for Korea, the Bangkok SET Index for Thailand, and the Morgan Stanley Capital International Index for Mexico.

[1]Correlation between squared daily local return and lagged squared daily return of the Dow Jones Industrial Average; ***, **, and * indicate significance at the 1 percent, 5 percent, and 10 percent levels, respectively. In addition, +++, ++, and + indicate a significant change in the correlation measure from the previous period at the 1 percent, 5 percent, and 10 percent levels, respectively.

---

on a net basis, $708 million of Hong Kong shares and set the stage for the rapid decline in share prices in the coming months. A similar reversal of capital flows occurred in Mexico. In February 1994, there was a net equity inflow of $280 million from the United States; however, in the following month, U.S. investors sold a net $170 million of Mexican shares. This rapid change in capital flows was accompanied by a rapid decline of stock prices in Mexico, demonstrating the important impact that volatile equity flows can have on the variability of stock prices in small local markets.

In this context, three related questions arise: Has the volatility of equity price changes increased in absolute terms in the emerging markets? Has this volatility increased in emerging stock markets relative to, for example, return volatility in the United States? Has the probability of large declines in stock prices increased? The results in Table 4-3 show that the absolute volatility of stock returns has shown little evidence of increasing during periods of increased portfolio flows, the exception being Hong Kong in the period when portfolio flows were very volatile.[62] In Mexico and Korea, absolute price volatility has actually declined.[63] The estimated declines in both absolute volatility and the probability of sharp price declines in Mexico and Korea do not support the view that increased portfolio flows will necessarily cause excessive speculative trading and price fluctuations. The decline in volatility may be due, in part, to an increase in liquidity associated with the inflow of capital. The relatively minor change in price volatility in the emerging markets generally reflects a similar pattern in the more developed equity markets throughout the world. For example, volatility in stock market returns in the United States declined during 1988–94. Despite this similarity, however, in all of the APEC emerging markets studied, there is strong evidence that the volatility of stock returns has increased relative to the volatility of stock returns in the United States, especially in the period when portfolio flows were very volatile. The most extreme case is Hong Kong, where the ratio of the standard deviation of stock returns in the volatile-flow period is more than twice that for the low-inflow period. This increase in relative volatility in the emerging markets is consistent with the view that volatile portfolio flows can magnify the sensitivity of stock returns in emerging stock markets to fluctuations in stock returns in the larger developed equity markets, such as in the United States.

With regard to the probability of sharp declines in stock prices, the most striking example is Hong Kong, where the probability of a price decline larger than 3 percent is about 10 percent in the volatile-flow-period and about 2 percent in the low-inflow period. In other markets, however, the probability of a sharp price

decline is not necessarily higher during periods with volatile flows. In Korea, the probability of a decline larger than 3 percent turns out to be lower in the volatile-flow period than in the other periods. For Thailand, the volatile-flow period has the highest probability of an extreme price drop. In Mexico, the probability of a sharp decline in the volatile-flow period is lower than in the low-inflow period but higher than in the more-steady-inflow period. Such sudden and sharp changes in prices and the risk of a sudden loss of liquidity (as discussed below) can significantly increase systemic risk.

Risk of a Sudden Loss of Market Liquidity

The rapid increase in foreign demand for emerging market equities combined with their relatively limited supply has fueled sharp increases in equity prices (Chart 4-1). The rise in stock prices was particularly pronounced during 1993 before easing somewhat in early 1994, as short-term interest rates in the United States moved upward. The surge in prices, in turn, has contributed to an important rise in market capitalization and an equally dramatic increase in price-earnings ratios (Table 4-5). For Mexico, the price-earnings ratio increased almost fivefold from 1988 to 1993, while those in Hong Kong and Thailand doubled from 1990 to 1993. This sharp run-up in prices and price-earnings ratios has fueled concerns about the impact of a reversal in the pattern of capital flows.[64]

A sudden withdrawal of funds by foreign investors can produce big variations in market liquidity, which in turn can lead to higher market volatility. This liquidity effect can be large, especially since, unlike the New York Stock Exchange in the United States, many APEC stock exchanges are operating on an auction/order-driven trading system without specialists or without securities dealers who will use their inventory to provide liquidity and smooth price fluctuations. The possibility of a sudden drop in market liquidity when it is most needed can imply that the benefits of the increase in portfolio flows in the form of a declining liquidity premium might not be fully realized.

---

[62]The increased volatility in Hong Kong may have been related to sudden reversals of investor sentiment about the prospects for investment in China.

[63]This is also true for Chile, another country that has been experiencing a surge in capital flows and a stock market boom; see Reinhart and Reinhart (1994).

---

[64]The experience of several Latin American countries during the late 1970s and early 1980s provides some basis for those concerns. In several countries, including Chile and Mexico, the surge in inflows was accompanied by booming equity and real estate prices; the abrupt reversal of those flows in the early 1980s eroded the earlier price gains and, in most instances, left stock prices well below their pre-boom levels; see Calvo, Leiderman, and Reinhart (1994). The impact of this reversal on financial markets and on the banking sector was substantial and is shown to have played a key role in spawning the banking crises that followed; see Rojas-Suárez and Weisbrod (1994). Similar, if less acute, adverse effects on the banking sector are also evident in industrial countries; see Schinasi and Hargraves (1993).

Chart 4-1. Stock Market Trends, January 1988–July 1994[1]

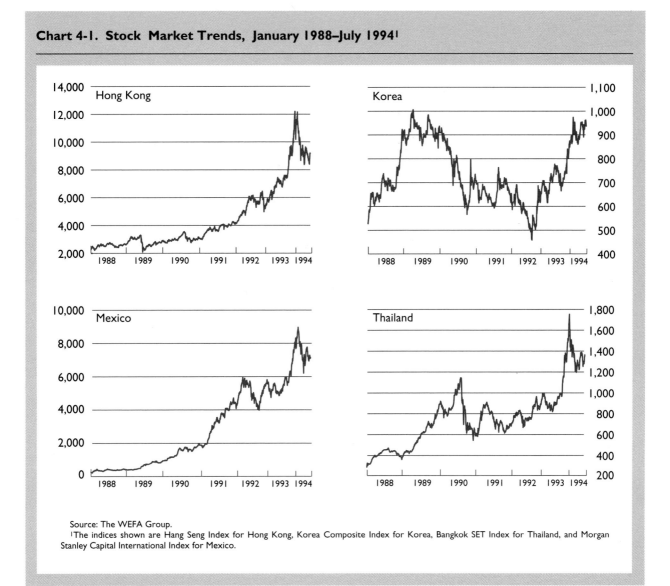

Source: The WEFA Group.
[1]The indices shown are Hang Seng Index for Hong Kong, Korea Composite Index for Korea, Bangkok SET Index for Thailand, and Morgan Stanley Capital International Index for Mexico.

Impact on Market Efficiency

On the positive side, as a result of the capital inflows, the efficiency of information in some recipient markets may have improved. Information efficiency allows capital markets to perform their allocative function by discovering prices of securities that reflect all available information. Mispricing may cause a misallocation of resources to relatively unproductive enterprises and industries, which will ultimately raise the cost of capital for efficient enterprises. The presence of international investors, who are often equipped with better valuation techniques and more advanced computer and information-processing technology, can speed up the adjustment of prices to changes in fundamental economic factors.

Market efficiency can be tested by examining the ability of local stock returns to predict future returns and by examining to what extent stock returns in industrial country markets (the U.S. equity market, for example) affect future equity returns in emerging markets (Table 4-6). The rationale for using predictability as a measure of inefficiency is that when stock prices are slow to adjust to new information, the ability of past stock returns to predict future returns is affected; likewise, changes in the speed of price adjustment can lead to changes in predictability. Greater predictability implies less efficiency. Predictability is examined both before and after the surges in portfolio flows and during both high-flow-volatility and low-flow-volatility episodes.

Table 4-5. Selected Stock Markets: Recent Developments
(In billions of U.S. dollars; end of period)

	1988	1989	1990	1991	1992	1993
Hong Kong						
Market capitalization	...	76.9	82.5	121.7	171.1	376.8
Price-earnings ratio	...	11.2	10.0	13.1	14.2	22.6
Number of listed companies	...	294.0	299.0	357.0	413.0	478.0
Korea						
Market capitalization	94.2	140.9	110.6	96.4	107.4	139.4
Price-earnings ratio	13.9	14.4	12.6	10.7	11.6	17.7
Number of listed companies	502.0	626.0	669.0	686.0	688.0	693.0
Thailand						
Market capitalization	8.8	25.6	23.9	35.8	58.3	130.5
Price-earnings ratio	12.0	26.4	13.8	15.6	16.3	26.1
Number of listed companies	141.0	175.0	214.0	276.0	305.0	347.0
Mexico						
Market capitalization	13.8	22.6	32.7	98.2	139.1	200.7
Price-earnings ratio	3.4	8.9	11.9	14.5	13.5	18.8
Number of listed companies	203.0	203.0	199.0	209.0	195.0	190.0

Sources: Asiamoney, *Asian Equity Guide* (March 1994); and International Finance Corporation, Emerging Markets Data Base.

As Table 4-6 shows, predictability using past local market returns (Column 1) is lower for Hong Kong and Mexico in the high-inflow and steady-inflow periods, respectively, than in the previous low-inflow period, which suggests greater efficiency. Predictability of Korean stock returns is essentially unchanged following an inflow of foreign capital. For Thailand, predictability by past local market returns is also high in the moderate-inflow period.

The tests of the predictability of emerging stock market returns using past returns from the U.S. stock market (Column 2) reveal that predictability is greater when portfolio flows are larger, especially when they are volatile. Using both past local market returns and the returns from the U.S. stock market (Column 3), predictability seems to be higher when flows have been volatile, suggesting that for all countries examined except Thailand, there was some loss of efficiency.

Role of the Financial Infrastructure

Although differences across markets may reflect differences in market fundamentals, it is unclear how portfolio investment by foreign investors alone could have produced major changes in the volatility of market fundamentals and in the cross-country relationships between market fundamentals. It is more likely that cross-country differences reflect fundamental differences in the underlying structure of equity markets in individual countries, and, in particular, differences in the underlying financial infrastructures.

The underlying structural characteristics of these emerging equity markets that are most likely to affect the relationships between portfolio capital flows and the determination of equity prices are (1) accounting and disclosure requirements; (2) the capacity of the trading systems; (3) the availability of derivative products, margin trading, and short selling; and (4) the clearance and settlement system in the equity markets.

Accounting and Disclosure Requirements

One fundamental reason for high price volatility in many APEC developing countries is a lack of information. When information is uncertain and disclosure is inadequate, unsubstantiated rumors cause volatility. Differences in the availability and quality of information and the speed with which it is disseminated can affect the impact of sudden changes in portfolio flows on both price and volume volatility, especially in relatively small and illiquid equity markets.

For example, the improvement in disclosure requirements in Thailand following the enactment of the Securities and Exchange Act in 1992 may explain the decrease in volatility spillover from the U.S. stock market, as well as the decline in the likelihood of extreme price movements as the portfolio flows increased. The adoption of the Automated System Stock Exchange of Thailand (ASSET), which, in addition to confirming orders also calculates market statistics and supports market surveillance and regulatory functions, would also have facilitated the dissemination of information to

Table 4-6. Market Efficiency Tests
(In percent)

	Predictability of Local Stock Market Return		
	Using past local returns	Using past Dow Jones Industrial Average (DJIA) returns	Using past local and DJIA returns
Hong Kong			
Low-inflow period (Jan. 1988–Aug. 1991)	6.5	6.4	13.2
High-inflow period (Sept. 1991–Oct. 1993)	4.3	4.1	8.0
Volatile-flow period (Nov. 1993–July 1994)	7.9	16.8	22.1
Korea			
Low-inflow period (Jan. 1988–Dec. 1991)	3.5	1.8	5.1
High-inflow period (Jan. 1992–June 1993)	3.9	3.1	7.1
Volatile-flow period (July 1993–July 1994)	5.3	3.0	8.0
Thailand			
Volatile-flow period (Jan. 1988–Apr. 1991)	3.6	14.2	15.7
Moderate-inflow period (May 1991–Oct. 1992)	7.4	4.5	12.2
High-flow-volatility period (Nov. 1992–July 1994)	5.5	4.8	9.9
Mexico			
Low-inflow period (Jan. 1988–Apr. 1990)	8.7	2.3	12.2
Volatile-flow period (May 1990–Jan. 1993)	6.2	17.2	20.7
More-steady-inflow period (Feb. 1993–July 1994)	4.4	10.2	14.0

Source: IMF staff calculations from The WEFA Group Data Base.

Note: Predictability is measured by the regression R-square from regressing daily local market return on returns from the past ten days. It represents the percentage of the variation in the daily local market return explained by returns from the past ten days. The separation of the overall sample into different subsample periods with different portfolio flow characteristics is performed by inspecting the monthly portfolio flow data from the United States to these emerging markets and the data on the changes in monthly flows. The separation is also jointly determined by the use of common structural-break test statistics including the CUSUM test statistics and the CUSUMSQ test statistics. The return data are the continuously compounded daily return from the Hang Seng Index for Hong Kong, the Korea Composite Index for Korea, the Bangkok SET Index for Thailand, and the Morgan Stanley Capital International Index for Mexico.

the public. This, in turn, contributed to an increase in the informational efficiency of the market. By contrast, although the disclosure of insider information in the Korean stock market seems adequate, the reporting of accounting information only recently became more useful when the requirement that consolidated financial statements be provided took effect. This relative lack of information, interacting with a sudden surge in portfolio flows, may well have increased the impact of foreign shocks on the Korean market and accelerated the spillover effects of equity market turbulence in the industrial country equity markets during periods of rapid changes in portfolio capital flows.

These observations suggest that, to reduce the potential for instability and to improve the allocative performance of the market, the availability and quality of information need to be improved. For example, securities commissions might issue more detailed guidelines concerning the material that should be included in financial statements and require the adoption of internationally accepted methods of accounting (see Harris (1994)).

In addition, rules for reporting insider trades and for the conditions under which insiders cannot trade are useful in maintaining investor confidence in the fairness of the market and in reducing the impact on market volatility of rumors on insider trades. These rules may be more important in developing countries than in industrial countries, because stock ownership is more concentrated and the interconnections among major business families are probably closer than in larger, more developed markets. Disclosure to the public of directors' and large shareholders' interests can also reduce the possibility of market manipulation and the greater volatility that it may entail.

Market Size and System Capacity

The effect that portfolio flows can have on an emerging stock market depends importantly on the size of the flow relative to the size of the market, and the capacity of the market to quickly process and absorb foreign orders and transactions. The magnitude of flows into individual stock markets relative to their size

Table 4-7. Portfolio Flow Versus Trading Volume
(In millions of U.S. dollars)

	Monthly Portfolio Flow from the United States					Average Monthly Trading Volume in 1993
	Oct. 1993	Nov. 1993	Dec. 1993	Jan. 1994	Feb. 1994	
Hong Kong	1,336	464	674	−708	−217	12,500
Korea	195	146	58	225	102	17,642
Thailand	21	82	37	−64	−7	6,684
Mexico	662	966	1,736	452	280	5,295

Sources: The monthly portfolio flow data are from the United States, Department of Treasury. Average monthly trading volume for Korea, Thailand, and Mexico are based on IMF staff calculations using data published in International Finance Corporation, *Quarterly Review of Emerging Markets: Fourth Quarter 1993*. Average monthly trading volume for Hong Kong is based on IMF staff calculations using data published in Asiamoney, *Asian Equity Guide* (March 1994).

may also help explain why the recent surge in flows affected individual markets differently.

Table 4-7 presents recent monthly figures for net equity inflows from the United States to those APEC markets studied. In October 1993, the net capital flow from the United States to the Hong Kong stock market was $1.3 billion, which was more than 10 percent of the average monthly trading volume in the market. In December 1993, the net portfolio flow from the United States to the Mexican stock market was $1.7 billion, about one-third its average monthly trading volume in 1993. The amount of portfolio flows relative to trading volume is also quite high for other months. It is important to note that because the portfolio flow figures are net figures (the difference between aggregate purchases and sales), the actual trading due to U.S. investors in these markets can be more than twice the amount of portfolio flows. As such, trading by U.S. investors in the Hong Kong and Mexican stock markets has contributed significantly to the total volume of trading.

In comparison, portfolio flows were small relative to trading volume in the Korean and Thai stock markets. These differences in the relative magnitudes of portfolio flows may explain the observations that both Mexico and Hong Kong have experienced the greatest volatility spillover effects from the U.S. stock market in the periods in which portfolio flows were volatile. The differences in the size of portfolio flows may also explain why the increase in local market volatility relative to that of the United States was the strongest for Hong Kong and Mexico when flows became volatile.

Derivative Trading, Margin Trading, and Short Selling

Some of the APEC developing countries have recently established derivatives markets. In Hong Kong, futures written on the Hang Seng index of 33 blue-chip stocks—the Hang Seng index futures—have been available for trading since May 1986, and the Hang Seng index options were introduced in March 1993. The introduction of individual stock options is planned for 1995. Trading in the Hang Seng index futures is very active: in the first three quarters of 1993, the turnover in the futures market was 1.3 times that of the spot market. Trading in the recently introduced index options is less active, with monthly trading volume reaching only 13 percent of trading in the index futures. It is often argued that derivative products, because they are highly leveraged, can also facilitate speculation, which can lead to higher stock market volatility and more extreme price movements. Hence, the availability of derivative instruments and program trading in Hong Kong may also explain why the Hong Kong stock market experienced the greatest increase in both absolute and relative volatility and a relatively high increase in volatility spillover effects when portfolio flows became very volatile.

A related issue is whether the market allows for margin trading (using borrowed funds to purchase an asset) and short selling (selling an asset one does not own, which results in a short position in that asset), which are other means of obtaining greater leverage. Hong Kong also allows margin trading, and the Securities and Futures Commission in Hong Kong does not impose direct restrictions on initial and variation margin levels.[65] In contrast, both Korea and Thailand have

---

[65]The only relevant (but minor) constraint in Hong Kong is the financial resources rule in the Securities Ordinances in which a broker's secured receivables may be counted as liquid assets only to the extent of the market value of the securities held as collateral. Generally, brokers operating in Hong Kong impose their own restrictions. The common initial margin level is 50 percent of the value of the collateral. Hong Kong also allows short selling as of January 1994, but only for some of the component stocks of the Hang Seng index. For borrowing of more than 14 days, a 15-basis point stamp duty is levied on both the borrower and the lender on top of the transaction stamp duty.

extensive margin regulations. In Korea, securities are classified into a margin group (for which margin trading is available) and a nonmargin group, and margin levels are determined by the Securities and Exchange Commission. The initial margin requirement is about 40 percent. Short selling is also allowed in Korea, but investors may short sell only up to 50 percent of their equity. To curb excessive margin trading and short selling, the commission also imposes limits on aggregate margin and short-selling positions. Specifically, total positions bought on margin for a stock may not exceed 20 percent of the total number of shares outstanding. Furthermore, total short selling is not allowed to exceed 10 percent of the total number of shares outstanding. In Thailand, margin trading is allowed, and maintenance and variation margin levels are set by the Securities and Exchange Commission of Thailand. However, one major difference between margin trading in Thailand and in many other countries is that margin payments must be made in cash—even highly liquid near-cash securities are not accepted.

In sum, the lack of margin regulation in Hong Kong relative to other countries might have facilitated the use of margin trading, which can potentially exacerbate market overreaction. This might also explain, in part, why the Hong Kong stock market was the market with the greatest increase in market volatility when portfolio flows became very volatile.

Clearance and Settlement

The proper design and implementation of clearing and settlement systems for stock transactions are essential for maintaining the ability of the emerging stock markets to absorb and allocate financial resources to their most productive uses, especially in the presence of large price fluctuations caused by rapid inflows and outflows of large amounts of foreign portfolio capital. The importance of having a properly designed exchange and clearing system with good risk management can be demonstrated by the experience of the Hong Kong futures market around the 1987 stock market crash.

In 1987, three organizations were involved with the risk management of the Hong Kong futures markets, but there were various problems with the prevailing arrangement. First, the clearinghouse was not involved in daily market monitoring and surveillance. Second, the guarantor could not set exchange membership standards including capital requirements. Third, the guarantor could not supervise the clearing members. Fourth, members of the Hong Kong Futures Exchange (HKFE) could not participate in the management of the clearinghouse guarantor. By 1987, the trading volume of the Hang Seng index futures had increased so much since its introduction in May 1986 that it exceeded the capacity of the system. These weaknesses almost led to

a collapse of the market in October 1987, when a big drop of the Hang Seng index caused many futures brokers to default. Trading was suspended for four days, and the Hong Kong Government, with the help of leading banks and brokerage firms, put together two HK$2 billion bailout packages to help the organizations meet their obligations. It was argued that in the absence of these packages the Hong Kong market would have collapsed.

This weak risk-management structure was replaced in May 1989 by a new clearinghouse, the Hong Kong Futures Exchange Clearing Corporation (HKCC), which provides both clearing and guarantee functions. Under the new structure, HKFE membership is a prerequisite for HKCC membership. Furthermore, a HK$220 million reserve fund was established, positions began to be expressed daily at current market values (marking-to-market), and the HKCC was given power to set margin requirements, make margin calls, and impose position limits. This new risk-management system held up very well during the market turbulence in June 1989 and in the early part of 1994, highlighting the importance of establishing adequate clearing arrangements.

The harmonization of settlement periods across markets is also important. Differences in the length of the settlement period across markets can impose additional settlement risk for international investors and can significantly affect their behavior and, hence, the behavior of market prices in the event of major market turbulence abroad. Furthermore, owing to differences in time zones, funding, and foreign exchange, a unilateral cut in the settlement period in one country can create settlement problems for international investors. In June 1994, the board of the International Securities Market Association (ISMA) unanimously decided that international securities transactions should be settled three days after trade execution (T+3) by June 1, 1995. Several APEC countries, such as Indonesia, Malaysia, and the Philippines, currently have longer settlement periods.

Conclusions

International capital markets have changed significantly in recent years, and these changes pose important challenges for the APEC developing countries. First, domestic banking systems must be well enough regulated and supervised to prevent a decline in credit quality in the presence of capital inflows. Second, domestic equity markets must be capable of coping with increases in market volatility and with possible spillover effects from turbulence in industrial country markets. Finally, the markets must have the integrity and transparency to retain the confidence of international investors even during periods of heightened uncertainties.

Improving the Banking Systems

To benefit fully from surges in capital inflows, APEC developing countries need to place greater emphasis on encouraging sound banking practices and on providing adequate supervision and regulation. In addition to medium-term measures to improve supervisory and regulatory frameworks, immediate action can be taken in several areas:

• The quality of bank supervision and regulation can be improved by credibly enforcing existing statutory limits that restrict commercial banks from engaging in activities that can be seen to have contributed to past crises, including large exposures to individual borrowers and related parties, or certain types of exchange rate and interest rate risk. Although beyond the scope of this paper, an evaluation of supervisory and regulatory enforcement by the authorities in individual countries would be helpful.

• Significant improvements in financial accounting and disclosure requirements would allow banks to assess and price credit risk more accurately. Moreover, the stability of the banking system would be improved if regulatory agencies, including central banks, had consistent access to detailed information about bank management, internal controls, and asset quality.

• Commercial bank loans extended to meet government-mandated quantitative targets are often risky and mispriced and have weakened bank balance sheets and financial systems in several APEC developing countries; economic policy objectives are best implemented directly and transparently rather than through commercial banks.

Improving the Domestic Equity Markets

Surges in portfolio flows have made it more likely that turbulence in developed capital markets will spill over into the APEC emerging markets. In fact, volatility in the APEC markets studied has increased relative to that of the United States, and this section has identified several potential weaknesses in the financial infrastructures that may have contributed to this increased volatility. Among the measures that these countries can take to strengthen their financial infrastructures are the following:

• Improving the quality and availability of information by adopting international accounting standards, including more timely, audited, and consolidated financial statements; disclosing transactions by large shareholders and insiders; collecting and disseminating information on prices and transactions as well as on takeover and acquisition activities; and coordinating disclosure rules across countries.

• Adapting trading systems to the increased volume and size of transactions to accommodate the increase in capital flows, and establishing mechanisms to reduce discrete price movements and variations in market liquidity, such as market makers (securities dealers that are prepared to trade at announced buy and sell prices).

• Enhancing risk management in clearance and settlement systems by improving market surveillance; adopting daily marking-to-market, imposing position limits, and setting proper margin requirements; strengthening capital adequacy standards for exchange and clearinghouse members; and harmonizing settlement periods to reduce the amount of risk in individual clearing systems.

• Limiting activity in derivative markets until a well-functioning infrastructure is established in primary markets. Without proper supervision and regulation, trading in derivatives can increase systemic risk.

Remaining Risks

These improvements will help reduce a country's vulnerability to the risks created by increased capital flows. However, even after adequate supervisory and regulatory frameworks are in place, appropriate policy actions may still be called for to address some other risks. First, capital inflows, which amounted to about 5 percent of GDP for all APEC developing countries in 1993, can be difficult to absorb without macroeconomic adjustments. Second, recent experience indicates that abrupt changes in capital flows can occur, leaving both private agents and policymakers little time to adjust. Third, even if banks are adequately regulated and supervised, nonbank financial institutions may remain vulnerable. Fourth, market concentration may be an important source of volatility and remains high in most APEC developing countries. The ten largest stocks accounted for between 28 percent and 68 percent of market value in 1993; this share was 14 percent for the United States. Even in the presence of these risks, however, the APEC developing countries can, with the proper mix of macroeconomic, financial, and structural policies, benefit from these capital inflows.

Appendix Elements of Commercial Bank Regulations in Selected APEC Developing Countries

Indonesia	Korea	Malaysia	Philippines	Taiwan Province of China[1]	Thailand

Ownership Regulations

Indonesia	Korea	Malaysia	Philippines	Taiwan Province of China[1]	Thailand
A corporation may own shares in a bank up to its own net worth.	No individual may own more than 8% of the voting stock of a nationwide commercial bank (15% for local banks).	Individuals may not own more than 10% of the shares of any financial institution.	An individual may not own more than 20% of the equity of a bank.	An individual investor may not own more than 5% of a bank's equity.	A bank must have at least 250 individual shareholders who together own no less than 50% of the shares issued.
Foreign ownership of traded shares of a domestic commercial bank may not exceed 49%.		Corporations may not own more than 20% of the shares of any financial institution.	A corporation may not own more than 30% of the equity of a bank.	A group of investors may not own more than 15% of a bank's equity.	An individual shareholder may own no more than 0.5% of a bank's shares.
Foreign banks may have a maximum equity participation of up to 85% of paid-up capital.		A corporation that is 75% owned by one family faces the ownership restriction applied to individuals.	A group of corporations that are majority-owned by the same group of persons may not own more than 20% of the equity of a bank.		An individual investor, the investor's spouse and children, and partners in a business activity may not own more than 5% of a bank's shares.
		The transfer of more than 5% of bank shares requires the approval of the Ministry of Finance.	Corporations that are majority-owned by an individual or family may not own more than 20% of the equity of a bank.		Thai shareholders must own at least 75% of a bank's shares.
			Foreign equity participation in a bank is limited to 30% of the voting stock of any one bank; foreign equity holdings may reach 40% of the bank's equity provided the excess over 30% is invested in nonvoting stock.[2]		
			These regulations do not apply to the ownership structures that were in effect in 1989, when the regulations were implemented.		

Capital Requirements

Indonesia	Korea	Malaysia	Philippines	Taiwan Province of China[1]	Thailand
Newly established private banks must have at least Rp 50 billion in capital.	Nationwide commercial banks must have minimum capital of W 25 billion; local banks must have capital of at least W 3 billion.	Commercial banks must have at least RM 20 million in capital.	Universal commercial banks must have capital of at least ₱ 1.5 billion; regular commercial banks with foreign currency unit licenses must have capital of at least ₱750 million.	Banks must have capital of at least NT$10 billion, of which at least 20% must be issued to the general public.	Banks' capital should equal at least 20% of their contingent liabilities.
Newly established joint venture banks must have at least Rp 100 billion in capital.	Equity capital must equal or exceed 5% of outstanding liabilities from credit obligations or guarantees.	Domestic banks must satisfy an 8% ratio of capital to risk assets according to a modified Bank for International Settlements capital adequacy framework.	Commercial banks are required to maintain a ratio of net worth to risk assets of 10% (8% for universal banks).	Banks must maintain a ratio of capital to risk-weighted assets of at least 8%.	Banks must maintain a ratio of capital to risk-weighted assets of at least 7.5%; of this, at least 5% must be tier I capital.
Banks must meet a minimum capital requirement of 8% of risk-weighted assets by December 1993.	Equity capital should exceed 7.25% of risk-weighted assets (8% by 1996).			Foreign banks must remit capital of at least NT$150 million plus NT$120 million per branch.	Foreign banks must maintain a ratio of capital to risk-weighted assets of at least 6.5%.
					Required minimum capital ratios increase to 8% for domestic banks (of which 5.5% must be tier I capital) and 6.75% for foreign banks at the end of 1994.
					Foreign bank branches must have assets of at least B 125 million in Thailand.

Appendix (continued)

Lending Restrictions

	Indonesia	Korea	Malaysia	Philippines	Taiwan Province of China	Thailand
	Commercial banks must allocate 20% of their credits to small businesses. Foreign banks may choose to allocate 20% of their credit to export-related activities. Banks must keep a loan/deposit ratio of less than 110%.	The volume of a bank's loans may not exceed its deposits. Nationwide commercial banks must allocate 45% of new loans to small and medium-sized enterprises. Foreign banks must allocate 45% of new loans to small and medium-sized enterprises. Banks make "policy" loans on the direction of the Government, financed by the National Investment Fund. Foreign currency loans may be extended only for the purposes of importing capital equipment, airplanes, used vessels, and high technologies, and of financing foreign direct investment abroad.	Lending to the Bumiputera community must equal or exceed 20% of end-1991 loans outstanding. Commercial banks must provide lending of at least RM 80 million under the Principal Guarantee Scheme; of this amount, RM 40 million must be made available to Bumiputera borrowers. Housing loan commitments must number 75,000 units with an aggregate value of RM 4,500 million, at a minimum interest rate of 1.75% above the base lending rate, or 9%, whichever is lower. The Ministry of Finance provides a 1% interest subsidy for loans made at 9%. Central bank or government-financed loans made, in part, through the banking system include the Fund for Food Scheme, the Fund to Accelerate Construction of Low-Cost Housing, and the Malaysian Shipping Finance Fund.	At least 75% of the total deposits, net of required reserves, and cash in vault accumulated in branches or banks in each of three regions outside the national capital region must be invested in that region. This condition may be considered satisfied if loans to agriculture and export industries equal at least 60% of deposits. Banks must set aside 25% of incremental loanable funds for agricultural lending as follows: 10% for agrarian reform beneficiaries and 15% for general agricultural lending. Banks must allocate 10% of their loan portfolio to small enterprises whose total assets amount to less than ₱5 million. Loans secured by real estate are limited to 70% of the property value; other secured loans are limited to 50% of the collateral value.	The volume of medium-term credit must not exceed the value of time deposits. Short-term credit facilities must not exceed the sum of time deposits and demand deposits. Medium banks must extend 70% of their loans to small and medium-sized enterprises. Building and construction loans may not exceed 20% of the sum of total deposits and bank debt instruments outstanding; construction loans must be for no longer than 20-year maturities. NT$ deposits of foreign banks may not exceed 15 times their remitted operating capital.	Banks must allocate at least 20% of credit to agriculture or other activities in rural areas. Once commercial banks commit themselves to 50% of the credit requested by priority sectors (at concessional interest rates), the central bank will provide the remaining 50%. Bank branches must extend credit equal to 60% of deposits to borrowers in that region.

Exposure Limits

	Indonesia	Korea	Malaysia	Philippines	Taiwan Province of China	Thailand

	1. Single-counterparty exposure limits apply to individuals and groups of related borrowers:[3]
	• New loans: 20% of bank capital
	• Old loans:
	
	Individuals *Groups* as of May
	20% 50% 1993
	            by end-Dec.
	20% 35% 1995
	            by end-March
	20% 20% 1997
	
	2. Other lending limits:
	• Parties related to the bank:[4] 10% of bank capital as of March 1997.
		1. Single-borrower limit:
		• Banks may not grant loans in excess of 20% of its equity capital to a single counterparty without approval from the Superintendent of Banks.
		• Banks may not lend to, guarantee, or assume the obligations of a single counterparty in excess of 40% of bank capital.
		• Each bank faces ceilings on its outstanding loans to the nation's 5 largest and 30 largest conglomerates.
		
		2. Other lending limits:
		• Banks may not lend to any of their officers or employees other than to make petty loans.
			1. Single-borrower exposure limits are prescribed by Bank Negara Malaysia; such limits apply to individual borrowers and their immediate family members, groups of borrowers acting in concert, and groups of affiliated companies.
			
			2. Other lending limits:
			• Loans to directors, officers, and employees and their family members, and companies in which any of these own more than 5% of the equity, except for the purchase of housing by family members, are prohibited.
			
			3. Foreign exchange exposure limits:
			• Net external liabilities of individual commercial banks, less
				1. Single-counterparty exposure limit applies to individuals and groups of affiliated borrowers:
				• The total of credits and contingent liabilities (minus loans secured by deposits or government securities) may not exceed 25% of the bank's unimpaired surplus and capital.
				
				2. Other lending limits:
				• Loans to directors, officers, shareholders, or related interests may not exceed an amount equal to their deposits and the book value of their paid-up capital contribution; unsecured lending
					1. Single-borrower exposure limits: information unavailable.
					
					2. Other lending limits:
					• The Banking Law of 1989 sets limits on related-party lending.
					• Banks may not extend credit to, or guarantee the obligations of, their directors or employees.
					
					3. Foreign exchange exposure limits:
					• The central bank sets ceilings on banks' foreign liabilities.
						1. Single-borrower limit:
						• Banks may not extend credit to any one individual borrower in excess of 25% of capital.
						• Banks may not offer off-balance-sheet commitments to any one customer in excess of 50% of capital.
						
						2. Other lending limits:
						• Banks may not extend loans or other obligations to their directors, their family members, or businesses in which they hold a 30% interest.

• Directors, commissioners, their family members, employees, and companies they own in which the ownership of the companies is 25% or more of the paid-up capital, whether individually or jointly: 10% of the bank capital.

• Shareholders or their family members or companies they own: up to 20% of bank capital if the shareholder's stake in the bank is less than 10%; up to 10% if the shareholder's stake in the bank is 10% or more.

• Companies owned by the bank: up to 10% of the bank's equity participation if the bank owns 25% or more of the company's equity; up to 20% of bank capital if the bank owns less than 25% of the company's equity.

3. Foreign exchange exposure limits:

• State-owned banks face a ceiling on their foreign liabilities; private banks must also report their foreign liabilities, but face no limits.

4. Investment restrictions:

• Banks may hold equity in banks or other financial institutions, such as leasing, venture capital, securities firms, insurance companies, and so on.

• Banks may conduct temporary equity participation to settle the problems of bad debt on the condition that in due time the equity participation shall be withdrawn.

• Banks may not grant loans for purposes of commodities or securities speculation.

• Banks may not grant loans to allow a customer to buy the bank's stock, or grant loans on pledge of its own stock or on stocks in excess of 20% of the equity of any other corporation.

• Banks may not grant loans to their subsidiaries in an aggregate amount exceeding 20% of capital.

3. Foreign exchange exposure limits apply to foreign exchange banks:

• The combined short and long positions may not exceed 10% of equity capital.

• The short spot position may not exceed 1% of equity capital or $2 million, whichever is higher.

• Documents proving underlying real demand for foreign exchange/won forward contracts with notional principal of more than the equivalent of $3 million and for periods longer than 2 working days must be provided within 45 working days of the initiation of the contract.

• Documents proving underlying real demand for foreign exchange/won futures contracts with notional principal above the equivalent of $10 million must be provided within 45 working days of the initiation of the contract.

4. Investment restrictions:

• Banks may not purchase or retain shares in any other bank.

• Banks may not purchase or retain shares in excess of 10% of the shares of any other corporation.

• Acceptance of shares and investments in bonds with maturities of more than 3 years shall not exceed 100% of the bank's equity capital.

• Banks may not possess real property other than that which is necessary for their operations; the value of such property may not exceed the bank's equity capital.

trade-related or investment-related inflows, are subject to a ceiling set by Bank Negara Malaysia.

4. Investment restrictions:

• Banks may not acquire shares in unrelated nonbank financial institutions or in other banks.

• Banks may invest in trustee shares or in shares of blue-chip privatized enterprises as prescribed by Bank Negara Malaysia.

• Banks may invest in non-trustee shares or interests in non-trustee shares of any corporation listed on the Kuala Lumpur Stock Exchange Main Board, subject to the following limits:

(i) Investments shall not exceed 5% of the corporation's paid-up capital or 5% of the banks' paid-up capital and published reserves (net working funds in the case of foreign banks).

(ii) The aggregate cost of investment in non-trustee shares may not exceed 5% of the bank's paid-up capital and reserves (net working funds in the case of foreign banks).

(iii) The aggregate cost of investment in trustee and non-trustee shares in Telekom, EON, and PROTON may not exceed 25% of the bank's paid-up capital and reserves (net working funds in the case of foreign banks).

(iv) Investments in shares of Telekom, EON, and PROTON will be subject to conditions (i) and (ii) above if these shares have not attained trustee status within 5 years of their listing.

• Banks may not acquire shares other than those provided above except in settlement of debts or through debt/equity swaps, and these must be disposed of within 12 months.

Other:

• Banks are prohibited from owning any immovable property other than that which is needed to conduct their business.

4. Investment restrictions:

• Banks may not own corporate securities or property other than that which is needed for their operations.

to such borrowers may not exceed 30% of their deposits and the book value of their paid-up capital.

• The aggregate of loans to directors, officers, shareholders, or related interests may not exceed 15% of the bank's loan portfolio, or 100% of its capital account net of deferred taxes and certain other adjustments.

3. Foreign exchange exposure limits:

• A bank's long foreign exchange position may not exceed 25% of the preceding month-end unimpaired capital; this measure is enforced daily.

• A bank's short foreign exchange position may not exceed 15% of the preceding month-end unimpaired capital; this measure is enforced daily.

3. Foreign exchange exposure limits:

• A bank's net foreign asset position may not exceed 25% of capital.

• A bank's net foreign liability position may not exceed 20% of capital.

4. Investment restrictions:

• A bank may not own shares or debentures of incorporated companies totaling more than 20% of total capital or 10% of the company's equity without approval of the Bank of Thailand.

• A bank may not own shares in another bank except those acquired in settlement of debts, and these must be disposed of within 6 months.

• A bank may not accept its own shares, or those of any other bank, as security for a loan.

• A bank may not own property other than that which is necessary for the conduct of its business or that acquired in the settlement of debts (which must be disposed of within 5 years).

Appendix (continued)

	Indonesia	Korea	Malaysia	Philippines	Taiwan Province of China	Thailand
Reserve Requirements	Banks must hold reserves of at least 2% of deposits in the form of cash on hand or a demand deposit with Bank Indonesia.	Banks must hold reserves equal to 11.5% of won-denominated demand, time and savings deposits, and residents' foreign currency deposits; and 1% of nonresidents' foreign currency deposits. Banks must maintain a minimum ratio of liquid assets to deposits of 30%.	Commercial banks face a statutory reserve requirement of 11.5% of eligible liabilities.	Banks must maintain reserves at the Bangko Sentral ng Pilipinas against deposits equal to 17% of eligible deposits; 55% of these reserves earn interest at an annual rate of 4%. Interbank loans have a 1% reserve requirement. Special time deposits under special financing programs of the government and Industrial Guarantee Loan Fund and Agricultural Loan Fund loans are exempt. Government-owned or -controlled banks must allocate 50% of their government deposits or other government funds in liquid assets.	Banks are required to hold reserve accounts with the central bank in the following proportions to deposits: • Checking deposits: 15–40% • Demand deposits: 10–35% • Savings deposits: 5–20% • Time deposits: 7–25% The central bank may mandate liquidity requirements.	Banks have a liquidity reserve ratio equal to 7% of total deposits: at least 2% must be held in interest-free deposits at the Bank of Thailand, no more than 2.5% may be held in cash, and the remainder must be held in eligible securities (government debt, Bank of Thailand bonds, and debentures and bonds of government organizations and enterprises).
Accounting for Asset Quality	Loan classification: 1. Current: a. Credit with installments other than house ownership credit: • No arrears in principal over 1 month, 3 months, and 6 months for credit with installment periods of less than 1 month, monthly/bimonthly/quarterly, and 4 months or more, respectively. • No arrears in interest over 1 month or 3 months for credit with installment periods of less than 1 month and 1 month or more, respectively. b. Credit with installments for house ownership: • No arrears in principal over 6 months.	Loan classification: 1. Normal: no delays in debt service longer than 3 months. 2. Precautionary: payments arrears of 3 to 6 months. 3. Substandard: that part of loans in arrears for 6 months or more that is adequately covered by collateral. 4. Doubtful: that part of loans in arrears for 6 months or more that is not covered by collateral but not yet loss. 5. Loss: doubtful loans for which collection is not expected.	Nonperforming loans: • Overdrafts in excess of approved limits, or of dormant accounts, for 6 months. • Term loans and revolving loans for which principal and interest payments are in arrears for 6 months. • Bankers' acceptances, trust receipts, and so on, that are not redeemed at maturity. • Rescheduled credits; if the loan was rescheduled before being classified as nonperforming then it is nonperforming if it is in arrears for a total of 6 months before and after rescheduling; if the loan was rescheduled after becoming nonperforming it remains classified as nonperforming until all arrears are cleared.	Loan classification: 1. Unclassified: currently performing; no expected payment difficulties. 2. Loans especially mentioned: currently performing, but potential exists for payment problems. 3. Substandard: loans under litigation; secured loans past due for 6 months but in the process of collection; unsecured loans past due for 90 days. 4. Doubtful: substandard loans without at least 20% repayment of principal during the succeeding 12 months; past due loans secured by collateral of declining value.	Loan classification: 1. Overdue loans: not repaid at maturity. 2. Called accounts: interest is 6 months overdue; or interest is less than 6 months overdue, but collateral is claimed by other creditors. 3. Bad loans: loans that are 2 years in arrears. For state-owned banks, the ratio of bad loans may not exceed 1% for secured loans and 3% for unsecured loans. Loans of state-owned banks are considered state assets; loan officers in such banks may be personally liable for loan losses.	Required loan-loss reserves: Banks must allocate 0.5% of deposits, borrowings, and other funds outstanding at the end of the previous year to the Financial Institutions Development Fund; these funds may be augmented by Bank of Thailand reserves.

2. Substandard:

Credit with installments other than house ownership credit:

• Principal arrears between 1 month and 2 months, 3 months and 6 months, and 6 months and 12 months for credit with installment periods of less than 1 month, monthly/bimonthly/quarterly, and 4 months or more, respectively.

• Interest arrears between 1 month and 3 months or between 3 months and 6 months for credit with installment periods of less than 1 month and 1 month or more, respectively.

Credit with installments for house ownership:

• Arrears in amortization of more than 6 months but not more than 9 months.

3. Doubtful: meets the criteria for neither current nor substandard, but collectible and the collateral value exceeds 75% of the debt or uncollectible, but the collateral value exceeds 100% of the debt.

4. Loss: does not meet the criteria for current, substandard, or doubtful; or meets the criteria for doubtful, but there has been no repayment or remedial action within 21 months of being classified as doubtful.

Required loan-loss reserves:

• Current: 0.5%
• Substandard: 3% after deducting collateral (10% after December 1996)
• Doubtful: 50% after deducting collateral
• Loss: 100% after deducting collateral

Required loan-loss reserves:

• Banks must allocate 10% of net profits to capital reserves until the latter equal the bank's paid-up capital.

• Banks must make loan-loss provisions equal to the expected loss for all loans.

• If a loan is charged off against loan-loss reserves, it must immediately be offset by an equal transfer to loan-loss reserves from net profit.

5. Loss: uncollectible or with worthless collateral; past due loans with no interest paid in 6 months; doubtful loans without at least 20% repayment of principal in the succeeding 12 months.

Required loan-loss reserves:

• Banks must set aside reserves equal to 1% of total loans less interest in suspense and specific provisions.

Required loan-loss reserves:
• Unclassified: 0%
• Loans especially mentioned: 0%
• Substandard: 25% of unsecured portion
• Doubtful: 50%
• Loss: 100%

Banks must have reserves equal to 10% of the book value of temporary investments in stocks and bonds.

Classification of other assets:

1. Real estate:

• Real estate is classified as substandard if held for less than 5 years; for real estate held more than 5 years, the reserve requirement increases by 10% each year held so that property held 10 or more years carries a reserve requirement of 50% (similar rules apply to personal property acquired except that the cutoff holding period is 3 years).

• The excess of book value over market value for real estate is classified as a loss asset.

2. Accounts receivable:

• Accounts receivable are substandard if 61–180 days old.
• Accounts receivable are doubtful if 181–360 days old.
• Accounts receivable are loss assets if more than 361 days old.

Appendix (concluded)

	Indonesia	Korea	Malaysia	Philippines	Taiwan Province of China	Thailand
Deposit Insurance	None	None	None	Philippine Deposit Insurance Corporation membership is compulsory for commercial banks. The maximum coverage is ₱100,000 per depositor.	Participation in the Central Deposit Insurance Corporation is voluntary; most private and public banks are not members; in June 1992, 39% of deposits were insured.	None

[1]Information may be incomplete owing to a lack of official contact with the authorities. In particular, recent financial liberalization measures may have changed some of these regulations.

[2]Upon implementation, the new law on foreign bank entry will allow three modes of entry for foreign banks: (1) the establishment of up to 10 new banks with full banking authority; (2) ownership of up to 60% of a new subsidiary; and (3) acquisition of up to 60% of an existing bank.

[3]Two borrowers are considered members of a group if (1) one company owns 35% or more of the equity of the other; or (2) a third party owns 35 percent or more of both companies; or (3) they have officers (e.g., directors) in common; or (4) one provides financial assistance to, or guarantees the obligations of, another.

[4]Parties related to a bank are shareholders who own 10% or more of the bank's paid-up capital; and bank commissioners, directors, their family members, officers, and companies, of which any of these own 25% or more.

Sources: *Answers to Essential Questions of International Banking and Securities Laws* (various issues) vol. I, *Asia* (1992); Bank Indonesia (various issues); Nasution (1993); IBCA Limited; Nam (1993); Bank of Korea (1990); Bank Negara Malaysia (various issues); Bloomberg Business News; Central Bank of the Philippines (various issues); Lamberte and Llanto (1993); SyCip, Gorres, Velayo & Company (various issues); Semkow (1992); Shea (1993); Bank of Thailand (various issues); and "Financial Sector Policies in Thailand" (1993).

References

Answers to Essential Questions of International Banking and Securities Law, vol. 1. *Asia* (London: Euromoney Publications, 1992).

Bank Indonesia, "Act of the Republic of Indonesia No. 7 of 1992 Concerning Banking with Regulations for Implementation" (Jakarta, Indonesia: The Bank).

Bank of Korea, *Financial System in Korea* (Seoul: The Bank, 1990).

Bank Negara Malaysia, *Annual Report* (Kuala Lumpur, Malaysia: The Bank, various issues).

Bank of Thailand, *Annual Report* (Bangkok, Thailand: The Bank, various issues).

Bercuson, Kenneth B., and Linda M. Koenig, *The Recent Surge in Capital Inflows to Three Asean Countries: Causes and Macroeconomic Impact*, Occasional Paper No. 15 (Kuala Lumpur, Malaysia: South East Asian Central Banks, 1993).

Calvo, Guillermo A., Leonardo Leiderman, and Carmen M. Reinhart, "Capital Inflows and Real Exchange Appreciation in Latin America: The Role of External Factors," *Staff Papers*, International Monetary Fund, Vol. 40 (March 1993), pp. 108–51.

———, "Capital Inflows to Latin America: The 1970s and the 1990s," in *Development, Trade and the Environment*, ed. by Edmar Bacha (London: McMillan, 1994).

Central Bank of the Philippines, *Annual Report* (Manila, Philippines: The Bank, various issues).

Cole, David C., "Financial Reforms in Four Southeast Asian Countries: Indonesia, Malaysia, Philippines and Thailand" (unpublished; Cambridge, Massachusetts: Harvard University, October 1993).

Feldman, Robert A., and Manmohan S. Kumar, "Emerging Equity Markets: Growth, Benefits, and Policy Concerns," IMF Paper on Policy Analysis and Assessment No. 94/7 (Washington: International Monetary Fund, March 1994).

"Financial Sector Policies in Thailand" (unpublished paper sumitted to and sponsored by the Asian Development Bank, October 1993).

Fischer, Bernhard, and Helmut Reisen, "Towards Capital Account Convertibility," Policy Brief No. 4 (Paris: Organization for Economic Cooperation and Development, 1992).

Harris, Ray, "Financial Disclosure and Accounting Standards" (unpublished paper prepared for the Asia-Pacific Forum on Securities Market Regulation and Supervision, Manila, Philippines, July 12, 1994).

International Monetary Fund, *International Capital Markets: Part II. Systemic Issues in International Finance*, World Economic and Financial Surveys (Washington: International Monetary Fund, 1993).

———, *International Capital Markets: Developments, Prospects, and Policy Issues*, World Economic and Financial Surveys (Washington: International Monetary Fund, 1994).

Kiguel, Miguel, and Leonardo Leiderman, "On the Consequences of Sterilized Intervention in Latin America: The Case of Columbia and Chile" (unpublished; International Monetary Fund, 1994).

Lamberte, Mario B., and Gilberto M. Llanto, "A Study of Financial Sector Policies: the Philippine Case" (paper prepared for the Conference on Financial Sector Development in Asia, Manila, Philippines, September 1–3, 1993).

Nam, Sang-Woo, "Korea's Financial Markets and Policies" (unpublished; Seoul: Korea Development Institute, October 1993).

Nasution, Anwar, "Financial Sector Policies in Indonesia, 1980–1993" (unpublished; University of Indonesia, October 1993).

Reinhart, Carmen M., and Vincent Reinhart, "Capital Inflows and Emerging Stock Markets" (unpublished; 1994).

Rojas-Suárez, Liliana, and Steven R. Weisbrod, "Financial Market Fragilities in Latin America: From Banking Crisis Resolution to Current Policy Challenges," IMF Working Paper No. WP/94/117 (Washington: International Monetary Fund, October 1994).

Schadler, Susan, Maria Carcovic, Adam Bennett, and Robert Kahn, *Recent Experiences with Surges in Capital Inflows*, IMF Occasional Paper No. 108 (Washington: International Monetary Fund, 1993).

Schinasi, Garry J., and Monica Hargraves, "'Boom and Bust' in Asset Markets in the 1980s: Causes and Consequences," in *Staff Studies for the World Economic Outlook*, World Economic and Financial Surveys (Washington: International Monetary Fund, 1993), pp. 1–27.

Semkow, Brian W., "Financial Reform in Thailand," *Butterworths Journal of International Banking and Financial Law* (June 1992), pp. 269–76.

Shea, Jia-Dong, "The Financial Development and Policies in Taipei, China" (unpublished; Nankang, Taiwan Province of China: Institute of Economics, Academia Sinica, October 1993).

Sudibyo, Bambang, and others, "Public Confidence on the Independence of Public Accountants" (paper presented in the Sixth Annual PACAP Finance Conference, Jakarta, Indonesia, July 6–8, 1994).

SyCip, Gorres, Velayo & Company, *A Study of the Commercial Banks in the Philippines: Annual Report* (Manila, Philippines: SGV & Co., various issues).

World Bank, *World Development Report 1994* (Washington: Oxford University Press, 1994).

Portfolio Capital Flows to the Developing Country Members of APEC

Appendix Tables

Table A1. Capital Flows to APEC Developing Countries by Country[1]
(In billions of U.S. dollars)

	1982	1983	1984	1985	1986	1987	1988	1989	1990	1991	1992	1993
APEC developing countries	27.9	14.3	10.0	14.3	8.2	2.3	−4.1	6.9	26.6	51.9	43.3	89.4
Asia	17.8	15.8	11.0	17.3	10.7	0.6	3.2	5.0	13.0	29.8	23.6	57.6
NIEs	5.5	3.7	2.7	2.3	−3.0	−8.5	−6.6	−10.0	−5.0	5.1	7.3	8.7
Korea	1.8	1.8	3.0	2.3	−2.6	−8.5	−3.4	−3.9	−0.7	6.1	7.5	8.8
Singapore	1.8	0.8	0.8	1.0	1.2	2.6	3.0	1.7	2.3	1.9	2.9	3.3
Taiwan Province of China	1.8	1.1	−1.1	−1.0	−1.6	−2.6	−6.3	−7.8	−6.6	−2.8	−3.1	−3.4
Other	12.4	12.1	8.4	15.0	13.7	9.1	9.8	15.0	17.9	24.7	16.3	48.9
China	0.4	—	−0.1	6.7	8.2	5.8	7.1	5.2	6.5	7.7	0.7	27.4
Indonesia	5.1	5.3	3.0	1.9	2.9	2.5	1.8	3.0	4.7	5.9	5.7	7.5
Malaysia	3.6	4.0	3.1	1.6	1.1	−0.5	−1.2	0.8	1.3	3.8	3.8	6.2
Papua New Guinea	0.5	0.3	0.2	0.1	0.1	0.2	0.2	0.3	0.2	0.3	0.2	0.1
Philippines	1.6	1.2	0.3	3.1	1.2	0.6	0.6	1.4	1.7	1.9	1.6	2.8
Thailand	1.2	1.3	1.8	1.6	0.1	0.6	1.3	4.3	3.6	5.1	4.2	4.9
Chile	1.7	−1.3	−0.7	−1.7	−2.6	−0.9	−2.1	0.1	0.8	0.5	0.8	1.5
Mexico	8.3	−0.3	−0.3	−1.3	0.1	2.6	−5.2	1.9	12.8	21.6	18.9	30.3
Memorandum items:												
Developing countries	62.1	38.0	36.6	23.7	9.0	−3.7	−6.0	1.0	12.6	57.1	52.7	104.8
Share of APEC developing countries in total private capital flows (in percent)	44.9	37.5	27.2	60.3	90.8	. . .	68.5	. . .	. . .	90.8	82.1	85.3

Sources: IMF, *Balance of Payments Statistics Yearbook*; and IMF staff estimates.

[1]Net medium- and long-term capital, excluding exceptional financing and flows related with debt- and debt-service reduction operations. Brunei and Hong Kong are not included owing to the unavailability of data.

Table A2. Net Foreign Direct Investment in APEC Developing Countries[1]
(In billions of U.S. dollars)

	1982	1983	1984	1985	1986	1987	1988	1989	1990	1991	1992	1993
APEC developing countries	5.6	4.4	4.5	4.2	6.0	8.2	8.5	8.4	12.1	19.1	23.4	39.5
Asia	3.6	3.8	4.1	3.6	4.8	6.1	6.9	4.5	8.9	14.0	18.7	34.1
NIEs	1.3	1.2	1.4	1.3	2.1	3.1	1.1	–3.0	–0.1	2.4	3.0	2.3
Korea	–0.1	–0.1	0.1	0.2	0.3	0.4	0.7	0.5	–0.1	–0.2	–0.5	–0.5
Singapore	1.3	1.1	1.2	0.8	1.5	2.6	3.5	1.9	3.9	3.2	4.3	4.3
Taiwan Province of China	0.1	0.1	0.1	0.3	0.3	—	–3.2	–5.3	–3.9	–0.6	–0.8	–1.5
Other	2.3	2.7	2.7	2.3	2.7	3.1	5.8	7.5	9.0	11.6	15.8	31.8
China	0.4	0.5	1.1	1.0	1.4	1.7	2.3	2.6	2.7	3.5	7.2	23.1
Indonesia	0.2	0.3	0.2	0.3	0.3	0.4	0.6	0.7	1.1	1.5	1.8	2.0
Malaysia	1.4	1.3	0.8	0.7	0.5	0.4	0.7	1.7	2.3	4.0	4.5	4.3
Papua New Guinea	0.1	0.1	0.1	0.1	0.1	0.1	0.1	0.2	0.1	0.2	0.2	0.1
Philippines	—	0.1	—	—	0.1	0.3	0.9	0.6	0.5	0.5	0.2	0.8
Thailand	0.2	0.3	0.4	0.2	0.3	0.2	1.1	1.7	2.3	1.8	2.0	1.5
Chile	0.4	0.1	0.1	0.1	0.1	0.2	1.0	1.3	0.6	0.4	0.3	0.4
Mexico	1.7	0.5	0.4	0.5	1.2	1.8	0.6	2.6	2.5	4.8	4.4	4.9
Memorandum items:												
Developing countries	22.4	13.4	14.3	10.7	10.3	11.6	16.7	16.2	21.4	28.3	35.4	51.6
Share of APEC developing countries in total foreign direct investment (in percent)	25.2	33.2	31.9	38.9	58.5	70.3	50.9	51.7	56.4	67.7	66.2	76.5

Sources: IMF, *Balance of Payments Statistics Yearbook*; and IMF staff estimates.
[1]Brunei and Hong Kong are not included owing to the unavailability of data.

Table A3. Net Portfolio Flows to APEC Developing Countries[1]
(In billions of U.S. dollars)

	1982	1983	1984	1985	1986	1987	1988	1989	1990	1991	1992	1993
APEC developing countries	2.0	0.1	−1.0	6.0	1.1	1.5	−2.5	0.8	0.5	11.5	19.9	37.1
Asia	1.1	0.7	−0.3	6.9	1.7	1.2	−1.6	0.3	−1.7	2.3	6.1	19.1
NIEs	0.1	0.2	0.1	1.1	−0.2	−0.2	−2.5	−1.0	−1.1	1.9	5.0	10.8
Korea	—	0.2	0.3	1.0	0.3	−0.1	−0.5	—	0.8	3.1	5.7	10.7
Singapore	—	—	−0.2	0.2	−0.5	0.3	−0.3	−0.1	−0.9	−1.2	−1.2	−0.1
Taiwan Province of China	0.1	—	−0.1	—	0.1	−0.4	−1.7	−0.9	−1.0	—	0.4	0.2
Other	1.0	0.5	−0.4	5.8	1.8	1.5	0.9	1.3	−0.7	0.4	1.1	8.3
China	—	−0.6	−1.6	3.0	1.6	1.1	0.9	−0.2	−0.2	0.2	−0.1	3.0
Indonesia	0.3	0.4	—	—	0.3	−0.1	−0.1	−0.2	−0.1	—	0.1	−0.1
Malaysia	0.6	0.7	1.1	1.9	—	0.1	−0.4	−0.1	−0.3	0.2	0.4	1.5
Philippines	—	—	—	—	—	—	—	0.3	—	0.1	—	−0.2
Thailand	0.1	0.1	0.2	0.9	—	0.3	0.5	1.5	—	−0.1	0.8	4.0
Chile	—	—	—	—	0.2	0.7	−0.1	0.1	0.4	—	0.3	0.7
Mexico	0.9	−0.7	−0.8	−1.0	−0.8	−0.4	−0.9	0.4	1.8	9.1	13.4	17.2
Memorandum items:												
Developing countries	−7.5	7.9	14.2	13.9	3.1	3.6	3.7	−1.0	2.2	16.8	33.2	55.0
Share of APEC developing countries in total portfolio flows (in percent)	...	0.7	...	43.2	34.4	43.1	...	...	21.1	68.5	59.8	67.4

Sources: IMF, *Balance of Payments Statistics Yearbook*; and IMF staff estimates.
[1]Brunei and Hong Kong are not included owing to the unavailability of data.

Table A4. International Bond Issues by APEC Developing Countries[1]
(In millions of U.S. dollars)

	1990	1991	1992	1993	QI	QII	QIII	QIV	QI	QII
					1993				1994	
APEC developing countries	3,833	6,755	12,136	31,072	4,435	7,769	5,267	13,601	10,514	6,460
Asia	1,356	2,773	5,916	19,856	2,230	3,300	3,416	10,910	7,207	5,070
NIEs	1,276	2,272	3,453	11,830	1,328	1,379	1,460	7,663	2,896	1,774
Hong Kong	66	100	185	5,887	657	—	692	4,538	1,305	550
Korea	1,105	2,012	3,208	5,864	671	1,343	725	3,125	1,273	580
Singapore	105	—	—	—	—	—	—	—	—	86
Taiwan Province of China	—	160	60	79	—	36	43	—	318	558
Other	80	501	2,463	8,026	902	1,921	1,956	3,247	4,311	3,296
China	—	115	1,359	3,047	406	751	1,209	681	1,500	872
Indonesia	80	369	494	485	30	—	—	455	699	750
Malaysia	—	—	—	954	—	500	—	454	230	735
Philippines	—	—	—	1,293	170	175	190	758	154	555
Thailand	—	17	610	2,247	296	495	557	899	1,728	384
Chile	—	200	120	433	—	333	—	100	—	—
Mexico	2,477	3,782	6,100	10,783	2,205	4,136	1,851	2,591	3,307	1,390
Memorandum items:										
Share of APEC issues										
Asia	35.4	41.1	48.7	63.9	50.3	42.5	64.9	80.2	68.5	78.5
NIEs	33.3	33.7	28.5	38.1	29.9	17.8	27.7	56.3	27.5	27.5
Other	2.1	7.4	20.3	25.8	20.3	24.7	37.1	23.9	41.0	51.0
Mexico	64.6	56.0	50.3	34.7	49.7	53.2	35.1	19.1	31.5	21.5
Total bond issues by developing countries	6,335	12,838	23,780	59,437	10,109	12,117	13,492	23,719	17,668	8,443
Share of APEC developing countries in total issuance by developing countries (in percent)	60.5	52.6	51.0	52.3	43.9	64.1	39.0	57.3	59.5	76.5

Sources: IMF staff estimates based on *Euroweek, Financial Times, International Financing Review, Financial Market Trends, Financial Statistics Monthly*, and data from the Organization for Economic Cooperation and Development.

[1] Including note issues under Euro medium-term note (EMTN) programs.

Table A5. International Bond Issues by APEC Developing Countries by Type of Borrower
(In millions of U.S. dollars)

	1990	1991	1992	1993	First Half 1994
APEC developing countries	3,833	6,756	12,136	31,073	16,972
Chile	—	200	120	433	—
China	—	115	1,359	3,048	2,371
Hong Kong	66	100	185	5,887	1,855
Indonesia	80	369	493	485	1,449
Korea	1,105	2,012	3,208	5,864	1,852
Malaysia	—	—	—	954	965
Mexico	2,477	3,783	6,101	10,783	4,697
Philippines	—	—	—	1,293	709
Singapore	105	—	—	—	86
Taiwan Province of China	—	160	60	79	876
Thailand	—	17	610	2,247	2,112
Sovereign borrowers	40	820	797	1,427	2,012
Chile	—	200	120	—	—
China	—	—	—	582	1,823
Mexico	40	620	377	352	—
Philippines	—	—	—	150	—
Thailand	—	—	300	343	189
Other public sector	2,686	2,029	4,783	12,752	5,158
China	—	115	1,359	2,443	548
Hong Kong	—	—	—	102	—
Indonesia	80	—	250	—	179
Korea	755	705	1,742	3,987	437
Malaysia	—	—	—	954	600
Mexico	1,851	1,192	1,432	4,401	3,240
Philippines	—	—	—	615	154
Thailand	—	17	—	250	—
Private sector	1,107	3,907	6,558	16,894	9,802
Chile	—	—	—	433	—
China	—	—	—	23	—
Hong Kong	66	100	185	5,785	1,855
Indonesia	—	369	243	485	1,270
Korea	350	1,307	1,466	1,877	1,415
Malaysia	—	—	—	—	365
Mexico	586	1,971	4,292	6,030	1,457
Philippines	—	—	—	528	555
Singapore	105	—	—	—	86
Taiwan Province of China	—	160	60	79	876
Thailand	—	—	310	1,654	1,923
Memorandum items:					
Share in total APEC issues (in percent)					
Sovereign issues	1.0	12.1	6.5	4.6	11.9
Other public issues	70.1	30.0	39.4	41.0	30.4
Private sector issues	28.9	57.8	54.0	54.4	57.8
Share of APEC issues in total developing country issues	60.5	52.6	51.0	52.3	65.0

Source: IMF staff estimates based on information from *International Financing Review*, *Euroweek*, and *Financial Times*.

Table A6. Yield Spreads at Launch for Unenhanced Bond Issues by APEC Developing Countries[1]
(In basis points)

	1990	1991	1992	1993	QI	QII	QIII	QIV	QI	QII
					1993				1994	
APEC developing countries	397	348	214	181	210	198	167	162	129	242
Asia	...	...	107	112	112	90	107	126	91	244
NIEs	...	...	108	94	107	83	86	96	67	79
Other	...	...	105	135	118	95	121	190	102	274
Chile and Mexico	397	348	314	288	317	293	277	263	175	227
Sovereign borrowers	...	186	152	130	197	...	94	88	89	98
China	...	...	...	88	...	...	89	88	94	98
Philippines	...	...	...	320	320	...	...	...	...	...
Thailand	...	...	100	67	57	...	74	...	54	...
Chile	...	150	150	...	...	...	...	...	...	...
Mexico	...	201	215	189	208	...	149	...	...	...
Other public sector	366	273	136	122	113	120	142	117	142	153
China	...	...	110	82	57	64	98	108	...	145
Indonesia	...	...	129	...	...	...	...	...	158	...
Korea	...	...	89	83	82	86	89	81	67	...
Malaysia	...	...	...	96	...	100	...	91	...	...
Philippines	...	...	...	250	...	310	265	217	178	250
Thailand	...	...	...	40	43	38	...	...	...	...
Mexico	366	247	205	192	190	182	213	187	154	126
Private sector	613	533	293	258	302	290	237	222	149	306
Hong Kong	...	...	180	118	133	...	83	126	...	115
Indonesia	...	...	...	410	500	...	...	405	...	467
Korea	...	...	116	87	86	76	90	92	68	69
Philippines	...	...	...	375	...	...	375	...	...	340
Thailand	...	...	43	60	...	58	...	75	127	94
Chile	...	...	...	194	...	210	...	170	...	...
Mexico	613	533	377	358	413	347	365	331	...	...
Memorandum items:										
All developing countries	245	346	282	259	288	274	249	243	187	259
Sovereign borrower	151	261	222	230	236	248	223	223	134	180
Other public sector	250	373	232	179	199	187	200	148	177	162
Private sector	650	493	376	348	424	370	339	315	256	337
Latin America										
(excluding Chile and Mexico)	449	455	426	400	581	481	332	371	306	360

Source: IMF staff estimates based on information from *International Financing Review, Euroweek,* and *Financial Times.*

[1]Yield spread measured as the difference between the bond yield at issue and the prevailing yield for industrial country government bonds in the same currency and of comparable maturity. All figures are weighted averages.

Table A7. Enhancements of International Bond Issues by APEC Developing Countries[1]

	1990	1991	1992	1993	First Half 1994
	(In percent of total number of issues)				
Number of issues featuring enhancements					
APEC developing countries	36	40	31	34	59
Convertible	10	32	14	25	48
Secured	19	4	9	3	2
Put option	10	6	17	13	29
Warrant	—	—	3	1	—
Asia	20	57	38	46	64
NIEs	21	51	38	51	79
Convertible	21	51	21	44	70
Put option	—	—	21	20	36
Warrant	—	—	10	1	—
Other	—	86	39	40	45
Convertible	—	86	30	34	34
Put option	—	29	30	19	30
Warrant	—	—	—	—	—
Chile and Mexico	44	18	24	13	30
Convertible	4	—	2	2	15
Secured	30	9	18	8	10
Put option	15	9	8	2	5
Warrant	—	—	—	1	—
All developing countries	27	33	22	25	48
Convertible	6	20	7	14	36
Guaranteed	2	1	1	2	3
Secured	14	4	7	3	3
Put option	6	9	12	11	22
Warrant	—	—	1	1	—
	(In percent of total funds raised)				
Value of enhanced bonds					
APEC developing countries	44	34	30	26	43
Asia	8	43	18	33	47
NIEs	9	35	16	38	62
Other	—	77	21	27	38
Chile and Mexico	64	28	41	13	30
All developing countries	31	31	20	21	43
Asia	7	39	18	35	50
Europe	11	—	8	1	5
Middle East and Africa	—	100	—	100	90
Western Hemisphere	59	34	26	12	23

Source: IMF staff estimates based on information from *International Financing Review*, *Euroweek*, and *Financial Times*.

[1]Totals by region may be smaller than the sum of their components because some issues feature multiple enhancements.

Table A8. International Bond Issues by APEC Developing Countries by Currency of Denomination

	1990	1991	1992	1993	First Half 1994
	(In millions of U.S. dollars)				
U.S. dollars	3,058	4,978	9,784	25,656	14,035
Asia	835	1,682	4,143	16,155	9,338
NIEs	755	1,347	2,848	10,133	2,899
Other	80	335	1,295	6,022	6,439
Chile and Mexico	2,224	3,296	5,642	9,501	4,697
Deutsche mark	345	299	388	174	205
Asia	135	96	125	—	205
NIEs	135	96	125	—	25
Other	—	—	—	—	180
Chile and Mexico	210	203	263	174	—
Yen	259	774	1,306	3,423	1,009
Asia	259	774	1,306	3,099	1,695
NIEs	259	659	317	1,262	1,035
Other	—	115	989	1,837	660
Chile and Mexico	—	—	—	324	—
Other currencies	170	704	659	1,818	1,037
Asia	—	221	343	602	1,037
NIEs	127	170	163	434	710
Other	—	51	180	168	327
Chile and Mexico	43	483	316	1,216	—
	(In percent of total)				
Memorandum items:					
Share in total issues by APEC developing countries					
U.S. dollar	80	74	81	83	83
Deutsche mark	9	4	3	1	1
Yen	7	12	11	11	10
Other	4	10	5	6	6
Share in total issues by developing countries					
U.S. dollar	61	68	71	74	81
Deutsche mark	27	13	8	8	3
Yen	7	11	15	13	10
Other	5	8	5	5	6
Share in total issues in global bond market					
U.S. dollar	32	30	39	36	37
Deutsche mark	8	7	11	13	7
Yen	14	14	13	12	13
Other	47	51	41	39	43

Source: IMF staff estimates based on information from *International Financing Review*, *Euroweek*, and *Financial Times*.

Table A9. International Equity Issues by APEC Developing Countries

	1990	1991	1992	1993	QI	QII	QIII	QIV	QI	QII
						1993			1994	
					(In millions of U.S. dollars)					
APEC developing countries	1,138	4,685	7,632	8,083	930	1,036	1,644	4,471	1,795	1,472
Asia	1,040	1,011	4,445	5,319	650	827	1,107	2,734	1,116	1,055
NIEs	254	465	2,215	2,277	443	393	250	1,191	292	428
Hong Kong	—	140	1,250	1,264	374	—	250	640	72	—
Korea	40	200	150	328	28	150	—	150	150	209
Singapore	214	125	272	613	41	171	—	401	70	—
Taiwan Province of China	—	—	543	72	—	72	—	—	—	219
Other	786	546	2,230	3,042	207	434	857	1,543	824	627
China	—	11	1,049	1,908	115	343	550	900	364	247
Indonesia	633	167	262	604	74	67	263	200	342	—
Malaysia	—	—	382	—	—	—	—	—	—	—
Philippines	53	159	392	64	—	—	44	19	2	—
Thailand	100	209	145	466	18	24	—	424	116	380
Chile	98	—	129	271	—	114	94	63	96	71
Mexico	—	3,764	3,058	2,493	280	95	443	1,674	583	346
Memorandum items:										
Share of APEC issues										
Asia	91.4	21.6	58.2	65.8	69.8	79.8	67.3	61.2	62.2	71.7
NIEs	22.3	9.9	29.0	28.2	47.6	42.3	15.2	26.6	16.3	29.1
Other	69.1	11.7	29.2	37.6	22.2	46.7	52.1	34.5	45.9	42.6
Mexico	—	78.4	40.1	30.8	30.1	9.2	37.4	32.5	23.5	28.3
Chile	8.6	—	1.7	3.4	—	11.0	5.7	1.4	5.3	4.8
Total equity issues by developing countries	1,262	5,436	9,259	11,865	1,000	3,200	2,351	5,312	3,823	3,090
Share of APEC developing countries in total issuance by developing countries (in percent)	90.2	82.2	82.4	68.1	93.0	32.4	69.9	84.2	47.0	47.6

Source: IMF staff estimates based on *Euroweek*, *Financial Times*, *International Financing Review (IFR)*, and IFR Equibase.

Table A10. International Equity Issues by APEC Developing Countries by Type
(In billions of U.S. dollars)

	1990	1991	1992	1993	First Half 1994
APEC developing countries	1,138	4,685	7,632	8,083	3,267
ADR/GDR[1]	99	3,688	4,185	3,306	1,430
Other	1,039	997	3,447	4,777	1,837
Asian countries	1,040	1,011	4,445	5,319	2,171
ADR/GDR[1]	1	238	1,009	677	578
Other	1,039	773	3,436	4,642	1,593
NIEs	254	465	2,215	2,277	720
ADR/GDR	—	200	693	435	578
Other	254	265	1,522	1,842	142
Other	786	546	2,230	3,042	1,451
ADR/GDR[1]	1	38	316	242	—
Other	785	508	1,914	2,800	1,451
Chile and Mexico	98	3,674	3,187	2,764	1,096
ADR/GDR[1]	90	3,449	3,176	2,700	852
Other	8	225	11	64	244
Memorandum items:					
All developing countries	1,262	5,436	9,259	11,865	6,913
ADR/GDR[1]	99	4,044	4,895	6,475	4,781
Other	1,163	1,392	4,364	5,390	2,132

Source: IMF staff estimates based on information from *Euroweek*, *Financial Times*, and *International Financing Review*.
[1] European depository receipts are included in ADR/GDR.

Table A11. Emerging Market Equity Funds Designated for APEC Developing Countries[1]
(Net assets in billions of U.S. dollars)

	Net Assets	Number of Funds	Net Assets	Number of Funds	Net Assets	Number of Funds	Net Assets	Number of Funds	Net Assets	Number of Funds	Net Assets	Number of Funds
	1988		1989		1990		1991		1992		1993	
APEC developing countries	2.7	35	4.5	62	5.3	101	6.7	119	9.2	197	16.9	231
Asia	2.4	34	4.0	58	4.4	93	5.2	110	7.3	185	13.9	219
NIEs	1.4	14	1.8	17	1.7	22	2.2	37	3.0	72	5.9	92
Korea	1.0	10	1.2	13	1.2	17	1.3	24	1.7	38	3.4	56
Taiwan Province of China	0.4	4	0.6	4	0.5	5	0.9	13	0.9	15	1.9	16
Other	1.0	20	2.2	41	2.7	71	3.0	73	4.7	113	8.6	127
China	—	2	—	2	—	3	0.1	4	1.3	34	3.2	48
Indonesia	—	1	0.3	7	0.5	18	0.4	18	0.4	21	0.9	22
Malaysia	0.1	3	0.2	7	0.5	17	0.6	17	0.6	23	1.0	21
Philippines	—	3	0.3	7	0.2	8	0.3	8	0.4	9	0.7	10
Thailand	0.8	11	1.4	18	1.4	25	1.6	26	1.9	26	2.9	26
Chile	—	—	0.2	2	0.4	4	0.7	4	0.9	4	1.1	4
Mexico	0.3	1	0.3	2	0.5	4	0.8	5	1.0	8	1.9	8
Memorandum items:												
Share of APEC developing countries in emerging market equity funds (in percent)	46.4	38.5	45.4	43.7	39.9	44.9	34.9	41.0	32.3	42.4	24.0	40.3
Total emerging market equity funds	5.9	91	10.0	142	13.3	225	19.2	290	29.2	465	72.5	573
Of which:												
Global funds	0.9	15	1.4	18	2.3	29	3.8	39	7.8	78	24.8	108
Asian funds	4.4	72	7.4	112	9.2	174	11.6	211	16.5	312	37.9	372
Of which: Regional	1.8	35	3.1	50	4.0	75	5.4	92	8.0	115	21.5	130
Latin American funds	0.5	4	1.0	9	1.5	16	3.5	33	4.5	64	9.1	78
Of which: Regional	—	—	0.2	2	0.4	5	1.5	18	2.0	40	5.2	53

Sources: Emerging Market Funds Research, Inc; and Lipper Analytical Services, Inc.
[1]Excludes Hong Kong.

Table A12. Net Equity Flows to APEC Developing Countries Through Emerging Market Mutual Funds[1]
(In millions of U.S. dollars)

	1989	1990	1991	1992	1993
APEC developing countries	−31	1,366	1,035	1,240	1,518
Asia	5	1,143	1,206	1,117	1,310
NIEs	83	775	779	1,001	1,146
Korea	160	407	352	342	1,131
Taiwan Province of China	−78	368	427	388	90
Other	197	1,469	107	835	57
China	−14	26	40	1,016	857
Indonesia	132	285	146	30	−35
Malaysia/Singapore	92	331	54	−64	−140
Philippines	131	302	−69	3	−84
Thailand	−145	525	−64	−150	−540
Chile	118	124	−13	7	−4
Mexico	−154	99	−158	117	213
Memorandum items:					
Share of APEC developing countries in emerging market equity funds (in percent)	...	21.1	41.2	13.7	10.3
Total emerging market equity funds	784	6,464	2,511	8,176	12,689
Of which:					
Global funds	−32	1,076	457	3,908	6,372
Asian funds	620	4,632	1,798	3,113	5,023
Of which: Regional	317	1,976	876	1,577	3,075
Latin American funds	120	652	57	738	1,403
Of which: Regional	106	185	267	446	1,320

Sources: IMF staff estimates based on data from Emerging Market Funds Research, Inc.; and Lipper Analytical Services, Inc.
[1]Excludes global funds and regional funds targeting Asia and Latin America; excludes Hong Kong.

Table A13. International Bond Issues by Country and Sector, 1990–June 1994

	APEC Developing Countries	Chile	Mexico	Hong Kong	Korea	Singapore	Taiwan Province of China	China	Indonesia	Malaysia	Philippines	Thailand
	(In millions of U.S. dollars)											
Financial sector	28,261	—	11,889	1,613	6,173	—	100	4,465	1,429	—	379	2,214
Banks	22,972	—	11,588	—	6,173	—	100	2,069	929	—	379	1,734
Other	5,289	—	301	1,613	—	—	—	2,396	500	—	—	480
Petroleum	5,333	—	3,927	—	250	—	—	—	—	954	90	112
Real estate	4,363	—	125	3,108	—	—	—	—	22	—	200	769
Utility	3,777	—	350	—	2,422	—	—	—	—	600	405	—
Cement	3,298	—	2,795	11	127	—	65	—	245	—	55	—
Manufacturing	2,190	—	1,140	550	470	—	—	—	30	—	—	—
Steel	2,134	—	220	183	1,576	—	—	—	—	—	—	154
Telecommunications	1,982	183	1,450	—	100	—	—	—	—	—	250	—
Electrical	1,820	—	235	150	1,007	—	383	—	—	—	—	45
Construction	1,784	—	860	185	347	—	43	—	—	230	—	120
Other[1]	15,828	570	4,848	2,293	1,570	191	584	2,428	1,151	135	623	1,572
Total	70,770	753	27,839	8,093	14,042	191	1,175	6,893	2,877	1,919	2,002	4,986
	(In percent of total)											
Financial sector	39.9	—	42.7	19.9	44.0	—	8.5	64.8	49.7	—	18.9	44.4
Banks	32.5	—	41.6	—	44.0	—	8.5	30.0	32.3	—	18.9	34.8
Other	7.5	—	1.1	19.9	—	—	—	34.8	17.4	—	—	9.6
Petroleum	7.5	—	14.1	—	1.8	—	—	—	—	49.7	4.5	2.2
Real estate	6.2	—	0.4	38.4	—	—	—	—	0.8	—	10.0	15.4
Utility	5.3	—	1.3	—	17.2	—	—	—	—	31.3	20.2	—
Cement	4.7	—	10.0	0.1	0.9	—	5.5	—	8.5	—	2.7	—
Manufacturing	3.1	—	4.1	6.8	3.3	—	—	—	1.0	—	—	—
Steel	3.0	—	0.8	2.3	11.2	—	—	—	—	—	—	3.1
Telecommunications	2.8	24.3	5.2	—	0.7	—	—	—	—	—	12.5	—
Electrical	2.6	—	0.8	1.9	7.2	—	32.6	—	—	—	—	0.9
Construction	2.5	—	3.1	2.3	2.5	—	3.7	—	—	12.0	—	2.4
Other[1]	22.4	75.7	17.4	28.3	11.2	100.0	49.7	35.2	40.0	7.0	31.1	31.5

Source: IMF staff estimates based on information from *International Financing Review, Euroweek,* and *Financial Times.*
[1]Includes sovereign issues.

Table A14. International Equity Issues by Country and Sector, 1990–June 1994

	APEC Developing Countries	Chile	Mexico	Hong Kong	Korea	Singapore	Taiwan Province of China	China	Indonesia	Malaysia	Philippines	Thailand
						(In millions of U.S. dollars)						
Telecommunications	4,651	98	3,159	—	—	401	—	—	—	251	316	426
Financial sector	3,339	71	1,092	1,607	—	82	—	93	206	27	49	112
Banks	1,652	71	603	595	—	82	—	—	200	—	5	96
Other	1,687	—	489	1,012	—	—	—	93	6	27	44	16
Manufacturing	2,779	—	1,082	—	49	—	—	1,460	124	—	55	9
Electronics	1,757	73	—	705	540	100	48	104	84	—	99	4
Media	1,516	—	1,516	—	—	—	—	—	—	—	—	—
Steel	1,248	111	30	—	—	112	400	509	—	—	—	86
Transportation	1,217	—	219	—	364	250	—	303	—	—	34	47
Real estate	791	—	—	250	—	—	—	102	227	—	72	140
Petroleum	631	—	—	—	—	40	—	342	—	—	—	249
Cement	461	—	461	—	—	—	—	—	—	—	—	—
Other	6,505	312	2,685	163	124	309	386	666	1,367	104	45	344
Total	24,895	665	10,244	2,725	1,077	1,294	834	3,579	2,008	382	670	1,417
						(In percent of total)						
Telecommunications	18.7	14.7	30.0	—	—	31.0	—	—	—	65.7	47.2	30.1
Financial sector	13.4	10.7	10.7	59.0	—	6.3	—	2.6	10.3	7.1	7.3	7.9
Banks	6.6	10.7	5.9	21.8	—	6.3	—	—	10.0	—	0.7	6.8
Others	6.8	—	4.8	37.1	—	—	—	2.6	0.3	7.1	6.6	1.1
Manufacturing	11.2	—	10.6	—	4.5	—	—	40.8	6.2	—	8.2	0.6
Electronics	7.1	11.0	—	25.9	50.1	7.7	5.8	2.9	4.2	—	14.8	0.3
Media	6.1	—	14.8	—	—	—	—	—	—	—	—	—
Steel	5.0	16.7	0.3	—	—	8.7	48.0	14.2	—	—	—	6.1
Transportation	4.9	—	2.1	—	33.8	19.3	—	8.5	—	—	5.1	3.3
Real estate	3.2	—	—	9.2	—	—	—	2.8	11.3	—	10.7	9.9
Petroleum	2.5	—	—	—	—	3.1	—	9.6	—	—	—	17.6
Cement	1.9	—	4.5	—	—	—	—	—	—	—	—	—
Other	26.1	46.9	26.2	6.0	11.5	23.9	46.3	18.6	68.1	27.2	6.7	24.3

Source: IMF staff estimates based on information from *International Financing Review, Euroweek,* and *Financial Times.*

Table A15. Net Purchases of Foreign Bonds by U.S. Investors
(In billions of U.S. dollars)

	1988	1989	1990	1991	1992	1993
APEC countries	−1.5	−1.3	−1.2	−6.6	0.3	4.8
Asia	−1.6	−1.2	−1.1	−6.9	−1.3	−1.4
NIEs	−1.2	−1.1	−1.2	−6.2	−0.5	−2.4
Hong Kong	−0.8	−0.8	−0.3	−4.1	−0.9	−1.9
Korea	−0.8	−0.2	0.2	0.7	1.5	1.8
Singapore	0.4	−0.1	−0.6	−0.4	0.5	0.2
Taiwan Province of China	—	—	−0.5	−2.3	−1.6	−2.5
Other	−0.4	−0.1	0.1	−0.7	−0.8	1.0
China	−0.1	0.1	−0.2	−0.4	−0.4	0.2
Indonesia	—	—	—	—	—	0.4
Malaysia	—	−0.1	0.3	−0.1	−0.5	0.4
Philippines	−0.2	−0.2	—	—	−0.2	−0.1
Thailand	−0.1	—	—	−0.1	0.3	—
Chile	—	—	−0.1	−0.2	−0.7	−0.1
Mexico	0.1	—	0.1	0.5	2.3	6.4

Source: U.S. Department of the Treasury, *Treasury Bulletin.*

Table A16. Net Purchases of Foreign Equities by U.S. Investors
(In billions of U.S. dollars)

	1988	1989	1990	1991	1992	1993
APEC countries	0.5	0.3	2.4	3.1	8.2	16.1
Asia	0.4	0.2	1.3	1.1	5.3	10.6
NIEs	0.2	0.2	1.1	0.9	4.6	8.9
Hong Kong	0.3	−0.3	0.6	1.1	3.6	6.3
Korea	—	—	—	—	0.5	1.3
Singapore	—	0.4	0.5	−0.2	0.5	1.2
Taiwan Province of China	—	—	—	—	—	0.1
Other	0.2	—	0.2	0.2	0.7	1.7
China	—	—	—	—	—	0.1
Indonesia	—	—	—	0.1	0.2	0.3
Malaysia	—	—	0.1	—	0.2	1.1
Philippines	—	—	—	—	0.2	0.1
Thailand	0.1	—	—	0.1	0.1	—
Chile	—	0.1	0.1	−0.1	0.1	0.3
Mexico	—	—	1.1	2.1	2.8	5.2

Source: U.S. Department of the Treasury, *Treasury Bulletin.*

Table A17. Portfolio Flows from Japan to Southeast Asia and China[1]
(In billions of U.S. dollars)

	1988	1989	1990	1991	1992	1993
Portfolio investment (net)	−5.3	−4.4	—	11.0	0.9	−0.2
Assets	−0.2	−0.5	0.2	−0.9	−1.1	—
Liabilities	−5.1	−3.9	−0.2	11.9	2.0	−0.2
Memorandum items:						
Medium- and long-term capital (net)	−13.4	−3.4	21.3	42.1	12.2	−1.0
Of which: Foreign direct investment (net)	−3.2	−5.5	−5.5	−3.2	−2.4	−2.1
Japan's current account surplus						
vis-à-vis Southeast Asia and China	17.4	11.9	14.2	28.8	39.6	54.6

Source: Japan, Ministry of Finance, *Zaisei Kinyu Tokei Geppo* (various issues).
[1]Southeast Asia comprises the Islamic State of Afghanistan, Bangladesh, Bhutan, Brunei, Hong Kong, India, Indonesia, Korea, Macao, Malaysia, Maldives, Myanmar, Nepal, Pakistan, the Philippines, Singapore, Sri Lanka, Taiwan Province of China, and Thailand. A minus sign indicates net outflows from Japan.

Table A18. Samurai Bond Issues by APEC Developing Countries
(In millions of U.S. dollars)

	1990	1991	1992	1993
APEC developing countries	242	586	1,145	2,401
China	—	260	829	917
Hong Kong	69	37[1]	—	—
Korea	173	290	316	719
Malaysia	—	—	—	450
Mexico	—	—	—	315
Memorandum item:				
APEC developing countries				
(in billions of yen)	35	79	145	267

Source: Japan, Ministry of Finance.
[1]Reflects a private placement.

Table A19. Net Purchases of Equities in Asian Stock Exchanges by Japanese Investors
(In millions of U.S. dollars)

	1992		1993		1994[1]	
	Net Purchases	Stock	Net Purchases	Stock	Net Purchases	Stock
APEC developing countries	−117	1,811	738	2,826	463	2,938
China	—	—	—	—	1	1
Hong Kong	84	1,033	432	1,380	199	1,402
Korea	—	—	—	—	—	—
Singapore	−156	526	3	694	57	713
Indonesia	−4	119	13	137	19	129
Malaysia	1	67	255	443	190	521
Philippines	2	1	2	5	1	2
Thailand	−44	65	33	167	−4	170

Source: Japan Securities Dealers Association.
[1] First seven months of 1994.

Table A20. List of Developing Country Stock Exchanges Designated by the Japanese Securities Dealers Association

Stock Exchanges	Date of Designation
APEC developing countries	
Hong Kong Stock Exchange	June 1, 1977
Kuala Lumpur Stock Exchange	June 1, 1977
Singapore Stock Exchange	June 1, 1977
Philippine Stock Exchange	June 1, 1977
Stock Exchange of Thailand	December 14, 1987
Jakarta Stock Exchange	December 26, 1989
Mexican Stock Exchange	June 28, 1990
Shanghai Stock Exchange	March 10, 1994
Shenzhen Stock Exchange	April 20, 1994
Non-APEC developing countries	
Buenos Aires Stock Exchange	June 17, 1992

Source: Japanese Securities Dealers Association.

Table A21. Net Assets of Emerging Market Country Funds Listed on the Osaka Securities Exchange
(In millions of U.S. dollars; end of period)

	Date Listed	1992	1993	1994[1]
Korea Fund	12/91	238	491	591
Korea Equity Fund	12/93	—	93	86
Morgan Stanley Asia Pacific Fund	8/94	—	—	751
Singapore Fund	12/91	51	118	116
Thai Capital Fund	12/91	72	134	125
Total		361	836	1,669

Source: Japan, Ministry of Finance.
[1] At the end of August.

Recent Occasional Papers of the International Monetary Fund

122. Capital Flows in the APEC Region, edited by Mohsin S. Khan and Carmen M. Reinhart. 1995.

121. Uganda: Adjustment with Growth, 1987–94, by Robert L. Sharer, Hema R. De Zoysa, and Calvin A. McDonald. 1995.

120. Economic Dislocation and Recovery in Lebanon, by Sena Eken, Paul Cashin, S. Nuri Erbaş, Jose Martelino, and Adnan Mazarei. 1995.

119. Singapore: A Case Study in Rapid Development, edited by Kenneth Bercuson with a staff team comprising Robert G. Carling, Aasim M. Husain, Thomas Rumbaugh, and Rachel van Elkan. 1995.

118. Sub-Saharan Africa: Growth, Savings, and Investment, by Michael T. Hadjimichael, Dhaneshwar Ghura, Martin Mühleisen, Roger Nord, and E. Murat Uçer. 1995.

117. Resilience and Growth Through Sustained Adjustment: The Moroccan Experience, by Saleh M. Nsouli, Sena Eken, Klaus Enders, Van-Can Thai, Jörg Decressin, and Filippo Cartiglia, with Janet Bungay. 1995.

116. Improving the International Monetary System: Constraints and Possibilities, by Michael Mussa, Morris Goldstein, Peter B. Clark, Donald J. Mathieson, and Tamim Bayoumi. 1994.

115. Exchange Rates and Economic Fundamentals: A Framework for Analysis, by Peter B. Clark, Leonardo Bartolini, Tamim Bayoumi, and Steven Symansky. 1994.

114. Economic Reform in China: A New Phase, by Wanda Tseng, Hoe Ee Khor, Kalpana Kochhar, Dubravko Mihaljek, and David Burton. 1994.

113. Poland: The Path to a Market Economy, by Liam P. Ebrill, Ajai Chopra, Charalambos Christofides, Paul Mylonas, Inci Otker, and Gerd Schwartz. 1994.

112. The Behavior of Non-Oil Commodity Prices, by Eduardo Borensztein, Mohsin S. Khan, Carmen M. Reinhart, and Peter Wickham. 1994.

111. The Russian Federation in Transition: External Developments, by Benedicte Vibe Christensen. 1994.

110. Limiting Central Bank Credit to the Government: Theory and Practice, by Carlo Cottarelli. 1993.

109. The Path to Convertibility and Growth: The Tunisian Experience, by Saleh M. Nsouli, Sena Eken, Paul Duran, Gerwin Bell, and Zühtü Yücelik. 1993.

108. Recent Experiences with Surges in Capital Inflows, by Susan Schadler, Maria Carkovic, Adam Bennett, and Robert Kahn. 1993.

107. China at the Threshold of a Market Economy, by Michael W. Bell, Hoe Ee Khor, and Kalpana Kochhar with Jun Ma, Simon N'guiamba, and Rajiv Lall. 1993.

106. Economic Adjustment in Low-Income Countries: Experience Under the Enhanced Structural Adjustment Facility, by Susan Schadler, Franek Rozwadowski, Siddharth Tiwari, and David O. Robinson. 1993.

105. The Structure and Operation of the World Gold Market, by Gary O'Callaghan. 1993.

104. Price Liberalization in Russia: Behavior of Prices, Household Incomes, and Consumption During the First Year, by Vincent Koen and Steven Phillips. 1993.

103. Liberalization of the Capital Account: Experiences and Issues, by Donald J. Mathieson and Liliana Rojas-Suárez. 1993.

102. Financial Sector Reforms and Exchange Arrangements in Eastern Europe. Part I: Financial Markets and Intermediation, by Guillermo A. Calvo and Manmohan S. Kumar. Part II: Exchange Arrangements of Previously Centrally Planned Economies, by Eduardo Borensztein and Paul R. Masson. 1993.

101. Spain: Converging with the European Community, by Michel Galy, Gonzalo Pastor, and Thierry Pujol. 1993.

100. The Gambia: Economic Adjustment in a Small Open Economy, by Michael T. Hadjimichael, Thomas Rumbaugh, and Eric Verreydt. 1992.

99. Mexico: The Strategy to Achieve Sustained Economic Growth, edited by Claudio Loser and Eliot Kalter. 1992.

98. Albania: From Isolation Toward Reform, by Mario I. Blejer, Mauro Mecagni, Ratna Sahay, Richard Hides, Barry Johnston, Piroska Nagy, and Roy Pepper. 1992.

97. Rules and Discretion in International Economic Policy, by Manuel Guitián. 1992.

96. Policy Issues in the Evolving International Monetary System, by Morris Goldstein, Peter Isard, Paul R. Masson, and Mark P. Taylor. 1992.

95. The Fiscal Dimensions of Adjustment in Low-Income Countries, by Karim Nashashibi, Sanjeev Gupta, Claire Liuksila, Henri Lorie, and Walter Mahler. 1992.

94. Tax Harmonization in the European Community: Policy Issues and Analysis, edited by George Kopits. 1992.

93. Regional Trade Arrangements, by Augusto de la Torre and Margaret R. Kelly. 1992.

92. Stabilization and Structural Reform in the Czech and Slovak Federal Republic: First Stage, by Bijan B. Aghevli, Eduardo Borensztein, and Tessa van der Willigen. 1992.

91. Economic Policies for a New South Africa, edited by Desmond Lachman and Kenneth Bercuson with a staff team comprising Daudi Ballali, Robert Corker, Charalambos Christofides, and James Wein. 1992.

90. The Internationalization of Currencies: An Appraisal of the Japanese Yen, by George S. Tavlas and Yuzuru Ozeki. 1992.

89. The Romanian Economic Reform Program, by Dimitri G. Demekas and Mohsin S. Khan. 1991.

88. Value-Added Tax: Administrative and Policy Issues, edited by Alan A. Tait. 1991.

87. Financial Assistance from Arab Countries and Arab Regional Institutions, by Pierre van den Boogaerde. 1991.

86. Ghana: Adjustment and Growth, 1983–91, by Ishan Kapur, Michael T. Hadjimichael, Paul Hilbers, Jerald Schiff, and Philippe Szymczak. 1991.

85. Thailand: Adjusting to Success—Current Policy Issues, by David Robinson, Yangho Byeon, and Ranjit Teja with Wanda Tseng. 1991.

84. Financial Liberalization, Money Demand, and Monetary Policy in Asian Countries, by Wanda Tseng and Robert Corker. 1991.

83. Economic Reform in Hungary Since 1968, by Anthony R. Boote and Janos Somogyi. 1991.

82. Characteristics of a Successful Exchange Rate System, by Jacob A. Frenkel, Morris Goldstein, and Paul R. Masson. 1991.

81. Currency Convertibility and the Transformation of Centrally Planned Economies, by Joshua E. Greene and Peter Isard. 1991.

80. Domestic Public Debt of Externally Indebted Countries, by Pablo E. Guidotti and Manmohan S. Kumar. 1991.

79. The Mongolian People's Republic: Toward a Market Economy, by Elizabeth Milne, John Leimone, Franek Rozwadowski, and Padej Sukachevin. 1991.

78. Exchange Rate Policy in Developing Countries: Some Analytical Issues, by Bijan B. Aghevli, Mohsin S. Khan, and Peter J. Montiel. 1991.

77. Determinants and Systemic Consequences of International Capital Flows, by Morris Goldstein, Donald J. Mathieson, David Folkerts-Landau, Timothy Lane, J. Saúl Lizondo, and Liliana Rojas-Suárez. 1991.

76. China: Economic Reform and Macroeconomic Management, by Mario Blejer, David Burton, Steven Dunaway, and Gyorgy Szapary. 1991.

75. German Unification: Economic Issues, edited by Leslie Lipschitz and Donogh McDonald. 1990.

74. The Impact of the European Community's Internal Market on the EFTA, by Richard K. Abrams, Peter K. Cornelius, Per L. Hedfors, and Gunnar Tersman. 1990.

73. The European Monetary System: Developments and Perspectives, by Horst Ungerer, Jouko J. Hauvonen, Augusto Lopez-Claros, and Thomas Mayer. 1990.

72. The Czech and Slovak Federal Republic: An Economy in Transition, by Jim Prust and an IMF Staff Team. 1990.

71. MULTIMOD Mark II: A Revised and Extended Model, by Paul Masson, Steven Symansky, and Guy Meredith. 1990.

70. The Conduct of Monetary Policy in the Major Industrial Countries: Instruments and Operating Procedures, by Dallas S. Batten, Michael P. Blackwell, In-Su Kim, Simon E. Nocera, and Yuzuru Ozeki. 1990.

Note: For information on the title and availability of Occasional Papers not listed, please consult the IMF *Publications Catalog* or contact IMF Publication Services.